W9-CLP-686

ALSO BY JOE SACCO

Palestine

Safe Area Goražde: The War in Eastern Bosnia 1992–95

Notes from a Defeatist

The Fixer: A Story from Sarajevo

War's End: Profiles from Bosnia 1995–96

But I Like It

Footnotes in Gaza

JOURNALISM

JOURNALISM

JOE SACCO

METROPOLITAN BOOKS HENRY HOLT AND COMPANY NEW YORK

Metropolitan Books
Henry Holt and Company, LLC
Publishers since 1866
175 Fifth Avenue
New York, New York 10010
www.henryholt.com

Library of Congress Cataloging-in-Publication Data

Sacco, Joe.
Journalism / Joe Sacco. — 1st U.S. ed.
p. cm.
"This volume collects most all the shorter reporting pieces I have done over the years for magazines, newspapers, and book anthologies. As such, it seems to call for some sort of introductory fusillade to rout all those who would naysay the legitimacy of comics as an effective means of journalism"— P.
ISBN 978-0-8050-9486-2
1. Military history, Modern—20th century—Comic books, strips, etc. 2. Military history, Modern—21st century—Comic books, strips, etc. 3. War—Comic books, strips, etc. 4. Society and war—Comic books, strips, etc. I. Title.
D431.S23 2012
355.0209—dc23 2011052079

Henry Holt books are available for special promotions and premiums.
For details contact: Director, Special Markets.

First U.S. Edition 2012

Designed by Kelly S. Too

Printed in China
10 9 8 7 6 5 4 3 2 1

To Paul Copley and Hal Swafford,
teachers and friends

CONTENTS

PREFACE

A MANIFESTO, ANYONE?

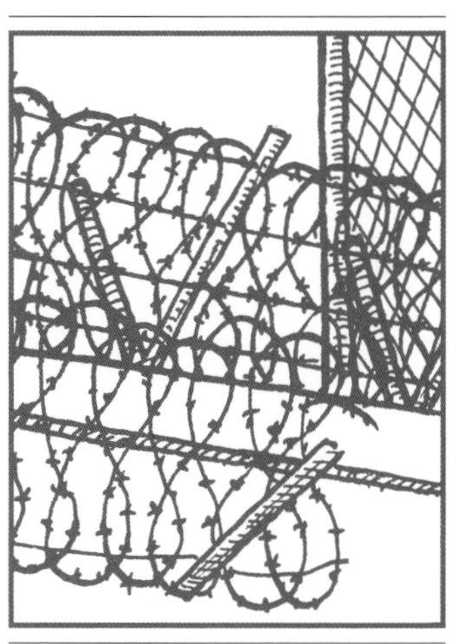

This volume collects most all the shorter reporting pieces I have done over the years for magazines, newspapers, and book anthologies. As such, it seems to call for some sort of introductory fusillade to rout all those who would naysay the legitimacy of comics as an effective means of journalism.

But before we commence firing, perhaps we should hear out the dissenters. After all, their objections may have merit. How should we respond, for example, when they question the notion that drawings can aspire to objective truth? Isn't that—objective truth—what journalism is all about? Aren't drawings by their very nature subjective?

The answer to this last question is yes. There will always exist, when presenting journalism in the comics form, a tension between those things that can be verified, like a quote caught on tape, and those things that defy verification, such as a drawing purporting to represent a specific episode. Drawings are interpretive even when they are slavish renditions of photographs, which are generally perceived to capture a real moment literally. But there is nothing *literal* about a drawing. A cartoonist assembles elements deliberately and places them with intent on a page. There is none of the photographer's luck at snapping a picture at precisely the right moment. A cartoonist "snaps" his drawing at any moment he or she chooses. It is this choosing that makes cartooning an inherently subjective medium.

This does not let the cartoonist who aspires to journalism off the hook. The journalist's standard obligations—to report accurately, to get quotes right, and to check claims—still pertain. But a comics journalist has obligations that go deeper than that. A writer can breezily describe a convoy of UN vehicles as "a convoy of UN vehicles" and move on to the rest of the story. A comics journalist must *draw* a convoy of vehicles, and that raises a lot of questions. So, what do these vehicles look like? What do the uniforms of the UN personnel look like? What does the road look like? And what about the surrounding hills?

Fortunately, there is no stylebook to tell the comics journalist how far he or she must go to get such details right. The cartoonist draws with the essential truth in mind, not the literal truth, and that allows for a wide variety of interpretations to accommodate a wide variety of drawing styles. No two cartoonists are going to draw a UN truck exactly the same way even if working from the same reference material.

Here I can only lay out my own standards as far as pictorial veracity is concerned. I try to draw people and objects as accurately as possible whenever possible. To my mind, anything that *can* be drawn accurately *should* be drawn accurately—by which I mean a drawn thing must be easily recognizable as the real thing it is meant to represent. However, there are drawings—particularly in scenes that take place in the past that I did not see myself—for which I must necessarily use my imagination, or, rather, my *informed* imagination. By this I mean that whatever I draw must have grounding in the specifics of the time, place, and situation I am trying to re-create. In film terms, a cartoonist is a set designer, a costume designer, and a casting director, and to successfully carry out those roles probably requires research in books, archives, and on the Internet. When relying on eyewitness testimony, I ask pertinent *visual* questions: How many people were there? Where was the barbed wire? Were the people sitting or standing? At the minimum I want to orient readers to a particular moment, but my goal is to satisfy an eyewitness that my drawn depiction essentially represents his or her experience.

But, as I have implied, this can hardly be a perfect undertaking. Ultimately, a drawing reflects the vision of the individual cartoonist.

I do not think this exiles a drawn report from the realm of journalism. I think it is possible to strive for accuracy within a drawn work's subjective framework. In other words, facts (a truck carrying prisoners came down the road) and subjectivity (how that scene is drawn) are not mutually exclusive. I, for one, embrace the implications of subjective reporting and prefer to highlight them. Since it is difficult (though not impossible) to draw myself out of a story, I usually don't try. The effect, journalistically speaking, is liberating. Since I am a "character" in my own work, I give myself journalistic permission to show my interactions with those I meet. Much can be learned about people from these personal exchanges, which most mainstream newspaper reporters, alas, excise from their articles. (The stories journalists tell around a dinner table, which generally involve similar interactions, are often more interesting and revealing than what gets into their copy.) Despite the impression they might try to give, journalists are not flies on the wall that are neither seen nor heard. In the field, when reporting, a journalist's presence is almost always felt. Young men shake their guns in the air when a camera crew starts filming, and they police each other when a reporter starts asking probing questions. By admitting that I am present at the scene, I mean to signal to the reader that journalism is a process with seams and imperfections practiced by a human being—it is not a cold science carried out behind Plexiglas by a robot.

This brings us to American journalism's Holy of Holies, "objectivity." To be clear, I have no trouble with the word itself, if it simply means approaching a story without any preconceived ideas at all. The problem is I don't think most journalists approach a story that has any importance in that way. I certainly can't. An American journalist arriving on the tarmac in Afghanistan does not immediately drop her American views to become a blank slate on which her new, sharp-eyed observations can now be impressed. Does she suddenly stop thinking of the American soldiers she is following as basically decent, well-meaning countrymen who share many of her values in order to assess them as instruments of a nation-state operating in its own interest as—objectively speaking—they are? At the very best, she tries to report on their actions and behavior honestly whatever her own sympathies. As the legendary American journalist Edward R. Murrow said, "Everyone is a prisoner of his own experiences. No one can eliminate prejudices—just recognize them."

Another trap promoted in American journalism schools is the slavish adherence to "balance." But if one side says one thing and the other side says another, does the truth necessarily reside "somewhere in the middle"? A journalist who says, "Well, I pissed off both sides—I must be doing something right," is probably fooling himself and, worse, he may be fooling the reader. Balance should not be a smokescreen for laziness. If there are two or more versions of events, a journalist needs to explore and consider each claim, but ultimately the journalist must get to the bottom of a contested account independently of those making their claims. As much as journalism is about "what they said they saw," it is about "what I saw for myself." The journalist must strive to find out what is going on and tell it, not neuter the truth in the name of equal time.

I've picked the stories I wanted to tell, and by those selections my own sympathies should be clear. I chiefly concern myself with those who seldom get a hearing, and I don't feel it is incumbent on me to balance their voices with the well-crafted apologetics of the powerful. The powerful are generally excellently served by the mainstream media or propaganda organs. The powerful should be quoted, yes, but to measure their pronouncements against the truth, not to obscure it. If I believe power brings out the worst in people, I've observed that those on the short end of the stick don't always acquit themselves well either, and I've endeavored to report that. I think the great British journalist Robert Fisk gets the equation about right: "I always say that reporters should be neutral and unbiased on the side of those who suffer."

In short, the blessing of an inherently interpretive medium like comics is that it hasn't allowed me to lock myself within the confines of traditional journalism. By making it difficult to draw myself out of a scene, it hasn't permitted me to make a virtue of dispassion. For good or for ill, the comics medium is adamant, and it has forced me to make choices. In my view, that is part of its message.

Joe Sacco
April 2011

JOURNALISM

THE HAGUE

ALL RISE!
And we all rise in Courtroom One at the International Criminal Tribunal for the former Yugoslavia in The Hague, the Netherlands, for the solemn moment and majesty of...
the WAR CRIMES TRIALS
This is History, baby, with a capital H, the first international war crimes trials since the Nuremberg court put the likes of Goering and Hess in the dock...
Written and drawn by JOE SACCO © 1998; Color by RHEA PATTON
But the judges striding in today haven't brought the victor's mighty gavel to crack down on a vanquished foe...
They've come with a United Nations mandate to sort through the crimes and atrocities committed by all sides in the recent Balkan wars.
The only other time I've been to court was to watch a friend argue down a traffic fine. But the accused at today's pre-trial motions, Dr. Milan Kovacevic, a Bosnian Serb hospital director, is in considerably hotter water...
Dr. Kovacevic is charged with genocide.
Genocide: Acts committed with the intent to destroy, in whole or in part, a national, ethnic, or religious group...
Genocide?
Him?
The prosecution says Kovacevic played a key role in setting up notorious camps—"transit centers," he once called them—as Serbs expelled Muslims and Croats from the Prijedor area at the beginning of the Bosnian War...
J. SACCO 6-98

The tribunal has already heard what went on in those camps at the trial of Dusko Tadic, a Bosnian Serb and former karate instructor...
Witness after witness described the living conditions...
the interrogations, the killings...
and the cases of sexual assault...
Q: "WERE YOU ORDERED TO LICK HIS ARSE, MR. H?"
"YES"
Q: "WAS MR. G ORDERED TO SUCK HIS PENIS?"
"YES"
Q: "WAS THE NEXT ORDER FOR MR. G TO BITE HIS TESTICLES?"
"YES"
BITE! HARDER! HARDER!
And Mr. G bit off the man's testicle.
The victim, Fikret Harambasic, wasn't the only Muslim savaged that day. Witnesses saw bloody bodies, a man being cut as "one slices chops," but the court said no deaths had been proven. It noted, though, that four of those assaulted, including Harambasic, were never seen again.
After the war, before he was nabbed by British soldiers, Dr. Kovacevic told a reporter—
WHAT WE DID WAS THE SAME AS AUSCHWITZ OR DACHAU, BUT IT WAS A MISTAKE.
IT WAS PLANNED TO HAVE BEEN A CAMP, BUT NOT A CONCENTRATION CAMP.
J. SACCO 6·98
One of his attorneys, Anthony D'Amato, a professor at Northwestern Law School, tells me that Kovacevic wanted to resign from the council overseeing the operation, but—
THEY SAID THEY WOULD SHOOT HIM.
HE HAD HEARD ABOUT THE ATROCITIES IN THE CAMPS.
HE DIDN'T WANT TO BE PART OF THE SCENE ANYMORE.

Neither Bosnian Serb leader Radovan Karadzic nor Bosnian Serb military commander Ratko Mladic, the two "most wanted" suspects, are here. They, too, are charged with genocide...

The tribunal is pursuing more familiar war crimes, like torture and murder, but is breaking new ground in its aggressive investigation of sexual assaults.
Prosecutor Patricia Sellers-Viseur tells me that, prior to these proceedings, war and rape were seen as virtually inseparable...
LIKE MAY SUNSHINE AND FLOWERS, LIKE SALT AND PEPPER.

The longer I'm in The Hague, the more I'm sucked into the courts' orderly deconstruction of some of recent history's foulest moments. I'm fascinated and stupefied by the sheer scope of the arguments, the expert witnesses droning on and on...
BLAH BLAH BLAH FRENCH REVOLUTION BLAH BLAH BLAH REVOLUTIONS OF 1848...

I can't stand the fact that trials are going on simultaneously, that I might be missing something more compelling at the one I'm not at...
BLAH BLAH NATIONAL BLAH
CAN WE DISMISS THIS WITNESS ALREADY?
DISINTEGRA BLAH BLAH

I'm silently cheering judges who are trying valiantly to prod their cases along...
DOES THE COURT NEED TO HEAR WHAT YOUR WITNESS DID FROM HIS BREAKFAST UPON ARRIVING IN BOSNIA TILL THE TIME THE FLAG CAME DOWN WHEN HE LEFT?
The tribunal is emphasizing pretrial management, has added courtrooms, and is petitioning the U.N. for more judges to help pick up the pace.

One of the tribunal's biggest problems, says Nikola Kostich, a former Milwaukee district attorney and a Serb-American defense lawyer, is the perception among some that its prosecution office is biased.
YOU HAVE LIMITED RESOURCES, BUT YOU HAVE TO SHOW RESULTS...
AND I THINK THEY TOOK THE EASY WAY OUT, AND THAT IS TO INVESTIGATE CERTAIN CRIMES AND CHARGE CERTAIN PEOPLE.
AND THE SERBS WERE THE ONES WHO ESSENTIALLY GOT HIT.

He ticks off the names of places where he says Croats and Muslims committed atrocities against Serbs.
Okay, but what about a certain U.N. report that pointed the finger squarely at the Bosnian Serbs?
YOU THINK ITS FINDING THAT SERBS COMMITTED GENOCIDE IN BOSNIA IS INCORRECT?
I THINK THE JURY IS STILL OUT ON WHO DID WHAT TO WHOM IN BOSNIA.
J. SACCO 6·98

But around a place called Srebrenica, the evidence still being dug up by investigative teams is mounting.
The massacre of thousands of Muslim men from there is a pivotal charge in the genocide cases against that elusive Dynamic Duo of War Crimes Suspects, Karadzic (whom Kostich has conferred with from time to time) and Mladic (who was "a lot of fun" when Kostich met him).
What did Kostich think happened in Srebrenica? After all, he himself had represented one soldier who'd confessed to personally executing up to 70 Muslims there...
MAYBE SOMETHING WAS DOWN THERE THAT WAS NOT GOOD.
THERE ARE NO HARD FACTS YET.
I MAYBE DON'T WANT TO BELIEVE IT EITHER, RIGHT?
I WOULD FEEL VERY SAD IF THIS OCCURRED THAT WAY. THAT WOULD BOTHER ME.
I'M A HUMAN BEING IN ADDITION TO BEING A DEFENSE ATTORNEY.
Ah, but a defense attorney is a defense attorney is a defense attorney. I ask Houston defense attorney Tom Moran about his Muslim client, who, among other things, is accused of killing an elderly Serb by nailing a political badge to his head. Is he innocent?
IT'S NONE OF MY BUSINESS...
WHAT I CARE ABOUT IS WHETHER THE PROSECUTOR CAN PROVE BEYOND A REASONABLE DOUBT WHAT'S IN THE INDICTMENT.
AND IF THE PROSECUTOR CAN'T DO IT, MY GUY IS NOT GUILTY.
DOESN'T MEAN HE'S INNOCENT.
J. SACCO 6.98
Anyway, he says his client was too small a player for an international court to be going after...
THE BOTTOM LINE IS, THIS TRIBUNAL WAS SET UP FOR TWO PEOPLE—RADOVAN KARADZIC AND RATKO MLADIC—AND THEY MAY VERY WELL BE INNOCENT...
AND UNLESS SOMEONE DOES SOMETHING TO GET THEM HERE, THIS TRIBUNAL MAY AS WELL PACK UP AND GO HOME.

The prosecutor's office insists it's building a case against the big fish by frying the smaller fish first. And the tribunal bigwigs don't buy the argument that success should be pegged to any couple of war crimes suspects, no matter how notorious.

The tribunal is dependent on others to apprehend suspects, and so it can't possibly bring every war criminal to justice — and now, with Kosovo erupting, it might have even more war crimes suspects to indict. Still, justice is worth pursuing for its own sake...
TRIBUNAL BUILDING
AND AT LEAST SOMEONE SOMEWHERE IS DRAWING THE LINE—IF ONLY A LEGAL LINE—ON CARNAGE AS WE STUMBLE OUT OF THIS CENTURY OF HORRORS.

But some say this tribunal and the one dealing with Rwanda exist today because of collective Western guilt.

For years we watched the butchery from our living rooms, and now that it's over we've dressed ourselves in robes and decided to do something about it after all.

Pronouncing the word genocide after the fact is a lot safer than stopping it.

It's like Bosnian lawyer Salih Karabdic, who survived the siege of Sarajevo, tells me—
SOMEBODY ORDERED IT, SOMEBODY DID IT, AND SOMEBODY TOLERATED IT.
AND ALL ARE GUILTY.
J. SACCO 6-98

And remember that testicle incident I told you about?
Well, the court determined that the accused, Dusko Tadic, was in the crowd of Bosnian Serbs cheering the scene that day.
They got Tadic on 11 counts, but that wasn't one of them...
ALL RISE!
After all, he was only watching.

The Hague, Notes

Details commissioned “The War Crimes Trials” during the short stint when Art Spiegelman was the magazine’s comics editor. I spent slightly less than two weeks at the International Criminal Court for the Former Yugoslavia in The Hague, the Netherlands, in May 1998. For me, the experience of watching the wheels of justice turn, however imperceptibly, was a satisfying cap to the reporting I’d done in Bosnia. Unfortunately, my visit to The Hague ended on a sour note. I had scheduled meetings with the two most important jurists involved in the war crimes trials at the time, Louise Arbour, chief prosecutor for both the former Yugoslavia and the Rwanda tribunals, and Gabrielle Kirk McDonald, president of the former Yugoslavia tribunal and a presiding judge, but they declined to do on-the-record interviews. My conference with them was a bizarre, demeaning episode. McDonald had obtained a number of my comics and had them on the table in front of her. Both she and Arbour had copies of *Details*, too. They insisted they did not object to a story about the tribunal in the comics form per se, but that *Details* magazine, with its glossy photos of spoiled young men and saucily clad women, was not an appropriate forum for an article about such serious matters as war crimes. McDonald read to me some brutal charges from a number of indictments to make her point. Forty-five minutes later, after using every argument I could think of to change their minds, they condescended to do the interviews if I would not quote them or attribute anything to them. In other words, they would talk to me only on background. This is why the last page of “The War Crimes Trials” is weak. It should have been the chief officers of the court who explained the great importance of the work being done at The Hague, not me.

“The War Crimes Trials” appeared in *Details*, September 1998.

THE PALESTINIAN TERRITORIES

WORLD

HEBRON: A LOOK INSIDE

An evil electricity crackles through the West Bank town—the sparks that arise when two peoples who hate each other rub together. TIME sent comic journalist **Joe Sacco** there for two weeks. He captured this fresh, provocative view

Colors by Rhea Patton

The taxis bringing us to Hebron can go no farther.

We jump out and make a run for the earthen barricade the Israelis have laid across the main road to hinder the movement of Palestinians.

We're lucky, says my guide Salem, 'cause usually Israeli soldiers are here to harass the people, but who wants to be out in this muck?

There's a slippery dash for taxis on the other side.

By the time we find one with room, 10 minutes later, we're soaked.

But the way to Hebron is now clear.

Hebron is the West Bank's most contentious town, the only one that's divided, the only one with Jewish settlers—who began to establish themselves in the late 1960's—living cheek by jowl with Palestinians.

In peace process-speak, the Palestinian Authority controls H1, 80% of Hebron; the Israeli military controls the rest, H2.

Let's face it, you have to be ultracommitted to move your family to the heart of a town whose 120,000 residents loathe you, and spokesman David Wilder and the 500 or so other Hebron settlers are just that. Originally from New Jersey, Wilder says it's "perhaps the climax of returning to one's roots" for a Jew to live here.

In the Israeli zone, the Tomb of the Patriarchs, Judaism's second holiest site, is underneath the Haram al-Khalil, Islam's fourth holiest place. For 700 years, until Israel occupied the West Bank in 1967, Jews were not allowed to worship inside. "If we were not here," says Wilder, "no Jew would get anywhere close to it."

"It's not a holy site for Jews," insists Nizar Ramadan, a writer associated with Hebron's fundamentalist Islamic movement. He says Israeli-imposed curfews and the other restrictions that often keep Muslim worshippers from the Haram are a "deep discrimination and a new kind of Nazism."

Many Palestinians charge the armed settlers and the soldiers who guard them with abuse and assault. Wilder charges back, "The Arabs are extremely good at lying."

In his view, it's the settlers—in their fortified compounds—who are under siege.

Jews had coexisted with Arabs in Hebron for hundreds of years until shortly after a massacre of 67 Jews by Arabs in 1929, and without the large Israeli army garrison to protect them now—

When shots are fired from H1 at the settlers, Israel punishes the 40,000 Palestinians under its control in H2 with a curfew.

The curfew can last months at a time, with breaks of a few hours only every few days.

The curfew prevents Majed Natshe from getting to his sweets shop job in H1. He's lost all his savings, he says.

He's been shot at three times while breaking the curfew in the back streets of H2, he says.

Wilder says the curfew is the—

Other bullets, February 1994: Mohammed Abu Ilhalaweh, a father of four, was at the Haram al-Khalil mosque when settler Dr. Baruch Goldstein from nearby Kiryat Arba walked in and killed 29 worshippers.

A gruesome photo on the wall reminds Abu Ilhalaweh of the bullet that paralyzed him that day, but—

and more than 30 "martyrs" in Hebron so far in this intifadeh.

RESULTS OF ISRAELI FIRE ON THE HARET AL-SHEIKH NEIGHBORHOOD, H1

If it's war, the settlers aren't satisfied with how the Israeli army is conducting it. When you're being shot at "from a particular source night after night, what do you do?" asks Wilder. "You level the house! Very simple to do... And they don't do it."

J. SACCO 1.01

Palestinians in Hebron have been killed in their homes. Fatina al-Fokhouri was wounded.

With one of the only English words he knows, her husband Sharif invites me to inspect where Israeli projectiles have punched through the walls.

Through an interpreter, I ask him if his home, which houses his extended family, was used by gunmen to shoot at the settlers.

Some of the positions from which Israeli troops fire are forcibly seized Palestinian rooftops in H2.

"We have to be where we have to be to prevent violence from the other side," Rasowicz says.

Israeli soldiers are on Izzi al-Sharabati's roof. He claims they've dumped garbage, urine and excrement on the rest of his house. He says this ceiling is crumbling because soldiers were moving and firing a heavy machine gun on top.

When he complained to the Israelis—

Attached as the settlers are to Hebron, any eventual peace deal will probably mean uprooting them. How? "Military force," predicts Amiram Goldblum, who tracks settlements for the Israeli protest movement Peace Now.

Meanwhile, Abu Ilhalaweh says his home is only half a kilometer from the grave of Dr. Baruch Goldstein, who was bludgeoned to death at the scene of the mosque attack. He says on the anniversary of Goldstein's crime and other occasions, settlers gather at the grave.

J. SACCO 1·01

GAZA PORTFOLIO

Sabha Abu Mousa searched for her daughter-in-law's two gold bracelets in the rubble of her home, which was demolished by the Israel Defense Forces, in the Khan Younis refugee camp.

Khan Younis refugee camp (left)

The Israeli checkpoint at Abu Houli that divided Khan Younis and the southern Gaza Strip from the north (below)

Palestinian fishermen cut off from the Mowasi enclave (which contained a Jewish settlement bloc) by an Israeli closure were unable to operate or maintain their boats and equipment for months.

Boys in Khan Younis followed a truck that announced the funeral of another "martyr."

Boys from the Khan Younis refugee camp moving up a dune toward an Israeli jeep. The soldiers taunted the children ("Come on, dogs!" and "Your mother's cunt!") and sometimes shot at them when they approached too close or threw stones.

The Underground War in Gaza

As the peace process lurches forward (and backward), towns like Rafah are still at war. A comic-book journalist reports on the battle over Palestinian tunnels and Israeli bulldozers.

By Joe Sacco

And this man, nicknamed Colonel Pinky, is charged with destroying them. He is the commander of the I.D.F.'s Southern Brigade of the Gaza Strip Division. The I.D.F. claims that "terrorists" sometimes slip through the tunnels, but mainly that they are used for smuggling.

Colonel Pinky judges his success by the price of a bullet in Rafah. The fewer the tunnels, the higher the price. He says a bullet now costs up to 21 shekels (about $4.50), the highest it's ever been. But that's not good enough, he says. He wants "zero smuggling in my area."

Colonel Pinky is taking me along the narrow Israeli-controlled corridor that divides Palestinian Rafah from Egyptian Rafah, an area so heavily bulldozed that rows of houses that once stood here have been ground down to sand.

More than 860 housing units have been destroyed since the beginning of this intifada, according to the Rafah governorate. The United Nations Relief and Works Agency (Unrwa), which provides aid to Palestinian refugees, puts the number at about 580 — but it counts even a multi-unit structure as a single house.

Colonel Pinky estimates that his bulldozers have demolished between 300 and 400 homes. (An I.D.F. spokesman in Jerusalem later tells me that only "a few dozen" of these were inhabited and suggests that the rest were "abandoned" or unfinished or perhaps sheds for animals.)

Colonel Pinky and I stand behind a 25-foot-high metal wall, which his forces are building as cover from Palestinian sniping. It also goes deep underground to create a barrier to the tunnels.

Houses are destroyed, he says, if they serve as "piers" for tunnels — more than 55 have been discovered so far, according to the I.D.F., sometimes hidden under tile floors or furniture — or if Palestinian militants use them to launch rifle, grenade or anti-tank attacks on his men.

One of his battalion commanders, Lt. Col. Avi, insists:

WE DON'T JUST RANDOMLY DESTROY HOMES.

To demolish a home, he says, he must submit a request that goes all the way up to the "legal adviser of the entire army." (According to the I.D.F., though, this procedure only applies to houses it considers "inhabited.")

J. SACCO 6-03

O.K., I say, let's talk about the destruction of one particular home. It belonged to someone I know—let's call him T.—and it was demolished not four days before, along with a few other dwellings.
Colonel Avi knows the houses. He says gunmen used them as cover to shoot at a bulldozer.
YOU CALL THIS A HOME, WE CALL THIS A MILITARY POSITION.
IT'S AN EMPTY HOME, A VACANT HOME THAT NO FAMILY IS LIVING IN.

The I.D.F. claim that houses demolished are mostly "empty" may be technically accurate, but Palestinians say that it turns the truth on its head. For example, T.'s home was "empty"—but only, he says, because he and his family were chased out by constant Israeli gunfire.
He visited his "empty" house every day, he says, and recently bricked it up so that gunmen couldn't use it.

The Israelis have succeeded in driving a wedge between the people living near the border and the gunmen. Though Palestinians here support the resistance in general, I've heard the gunmen called "useless," even "collaborators," because their ineffective attacks often invite a crushing Israeli response.
I've seen armed men chased off by a man who didn't want them lurking near his house.

Keeping the gunmen out is the "main reason" Fuad stays in his family home near the border despite the entreaties of his parents. The Israelis, he says—
—DON'T NEED AN EXCUSE TO DEMOLISH YOUR HOUSE, BUT THEY CAN USE THE GUNMEN AS A REASON.
While his watchful presence in his home would seem to satisfy the interests of the I.D.F., he says Israeli bullets still hit the house randomly. (I was present during one incident.) Palestinians typically interpret that message as an injunction to flee.

As for the tunnels, the reaction of Sami and his neighbors is precisely what the I.D.F. may have intended all along.
He shows me a tunnel entrance that they had completely blocked up with rubble.
WE DESTROYED THIS HOUSE BECAUSE OF A TUNNEL.
Sami says he and his neighbors "attacked" the smugglers who started this tunnel and chased them away.

He claims a smuggler offered him $60,000 to use his house to build a tunnel—
—AND I REALIZED IT WOULD NOT BE FOR GUNS OR WEAPONS, BUT FOR DRUGS.
I COULD HAVE BEEN A RICH MAN IN ONE NIGHT.
But he says he wants nothing to do with the smugglers. He doesn't want to give the Israelis an excuse to destroy his home.
J. SACCO 6-03

But even so, he can't be sure it will be spared. He says he believes the Israelis are using the issue of tunnels to extend the area they control along the border.

On the edge of Block J, he points to a site where the Israelis found a tunnel—

—150 METERS FROM HERE! SO WHY DID THEY DESTROY THIS WHOLE AREA?

One Palestinian militant I talk to admits that the I.D.F. has been about "90 percent successful" in its efforts to destroy tunnels, but:

NOW WE ARE NOT SO DEPENDENT ON THE TUNNELS AND ON EGYPT.

WITH A FEW MATERIALS AVAILABLE HERE, SUGAR, FOR EXAMPLE, OR FERTILIZER, I CAN CREATE VERY POWERFUL EXPLOSIVE MATERIAL.

He tells me Palestinians are even manufacturing bullets—not as good as "Russian" bullets, he says, but bullets just the same.

I ask Colonel Pinky when the demolitions in Rafah will stop. When "there is no resistance and there is no shooting," he says. "We want the tunnels to be stopped."

All things considered, he characterizes the Israeli response to Palestinian resistance and the tunnels as "gentle, if you can say gentle about something like this." If I wanted to see an army without restraint, he says, I should "go to Chechnya."

Such distinctions may be lost on the 5,300 people Unrwa says have lost their homes here. But T. doesn't seem bitter yet about the destruction of the house that he says he "spent all my life dreaming about."

In fact, after agonizing for weeks as the bulldozers drew nearer, he seems almost relieved now that the deed is done.

YES, BEFORE I HAD HOPE, BUT NOW IT'S FINISHED.

J. SACCO 6.03

Incidentally, when I returned to Block O to look up the woman who had asked me what I would do in her place, I didn't find her.

The whole row of houses, including hers, was gone.

The Palestinian Territories, Notes

I think of "Hebron: A Look Inside," which appeared in *Time* magazine, as my least successful piece of comics journalism. I cannot blame the senior editor, Joshua Cooper Ramo, who took a chance on comics journalism and supported me every step of the way. Working for that storied publication seemed to freeze me up, and I dispensed with my more typical first-person approach and reverted to the objective, tit-for-tat reporting I'd learned in journalism school. For this reason, I failed to adequately convey the great unfairness of making the free movement of tens of thousands of Palestinians hostage to the considerations of the few hundred militant Jewish settlers.

"Gaza Portfolio" includes both published and unpublished drawings meant to accompany an article my friend and colleague Chris Hedges wrote about Khan Younis, a town and refugee camp in the Gaza Strip. We sold ourselves as a team to Lewis Lapham, editor of *Harper's Magazine* at the time, and he commissioned our weeklong trip to Gaza. Unfortunately, I don't think Mr. Lapham appreciated what I could possibly add to Chris's article with drawings, and he seemed dissatisfied with the ones that showed human faces. I was put off by his second-guessing and almost abandoned the project. As it was, the few drawings published were printed so small as to induce further despair.

I consider "The Underground War in Gaza" a successful project even though, like the *Time* piece about Hebron, I was given only four pages. Representing the *New York Times Magazine* opened doors for me at the Israeli Foreign Press Office, and Israeli spokespersons asked if I would like to spend a day and night with Israel Defense Forces soldiers manning their positions along the Egyptian border. That opportunity allowed me to convey Israeli concerns about weapons smuggling while still questioning the enormous scale of the IDF's home-demolition campaign. Readers of my book *Footnotes in Gaza* might note that the "T" character whose home had just been demolished is Talal, the father of Ashraf, one of that book's main protagonists. Though I have nothing but good things to say about the editor who commissioned the piece, Paul Tough, the story passed through many hands, and there was some effort to get me to comply with the abbreviation commandments of the *New York Times* style guide. Additionally, I had to assure one editor that the background crosshatching on the second panel of the story's last page was not an effort to slip in a lot of little crucifixes.

"Hebron: A Look Inside" appeared in *Time*, March 12, 2001.

Only two of the illustrations shown in "Gaza Portfolio" ("The Khan Younis refugee camp" and "The Israeli checkpoint...") accompanied the article by Chris Hedges, "A Gaza Diary," in *Harper's Magazine*, October 2001; one illustration, "Sabha Abu Mousa...", appeared in a revised form (without the female figure); none of the other illustrations were used.

"The Underground War in Gaza" appeared in the *New York Times Magazine*, July 6, 2003.

THE CAUCASUS

CHECHEN WAR, CHECHEN WOMEN

I. GOING HOME

No no!
It's all right!
Easy does it!
No one is sending you back anywhere!
The poor thing has seen my bodyguards, which are required for foreigners traveling here, and thinks they are soldiers who've come to carry her back to the war zone.

Okay!
Everything is under control!
Her name is Zura, and she gets it now.
My translator has explained I come in peace.

In her tent, Zura tells me how she'd fled the war in Chechnya and has been living here as an "Internally Displaced Person" (I.D.P.) in the neighboring Russian republic of Ingushetia, in poor conditions but in safety, when—
I HEARD WOMEN SAYING THAT THE ONES THAT GO BACK TO CHECHNYA WILL BE PROVIDED WITH ACCOMMODATION AND HUMANITARIAN AID.

And Zura bought it.
She did precisely what the Russian authorities wanted her to do. She got on a bus and returned to Chechnya.
In Sernovodsk she was shown her new home, a room in an old technical school. But—
J. SACCO 9.03

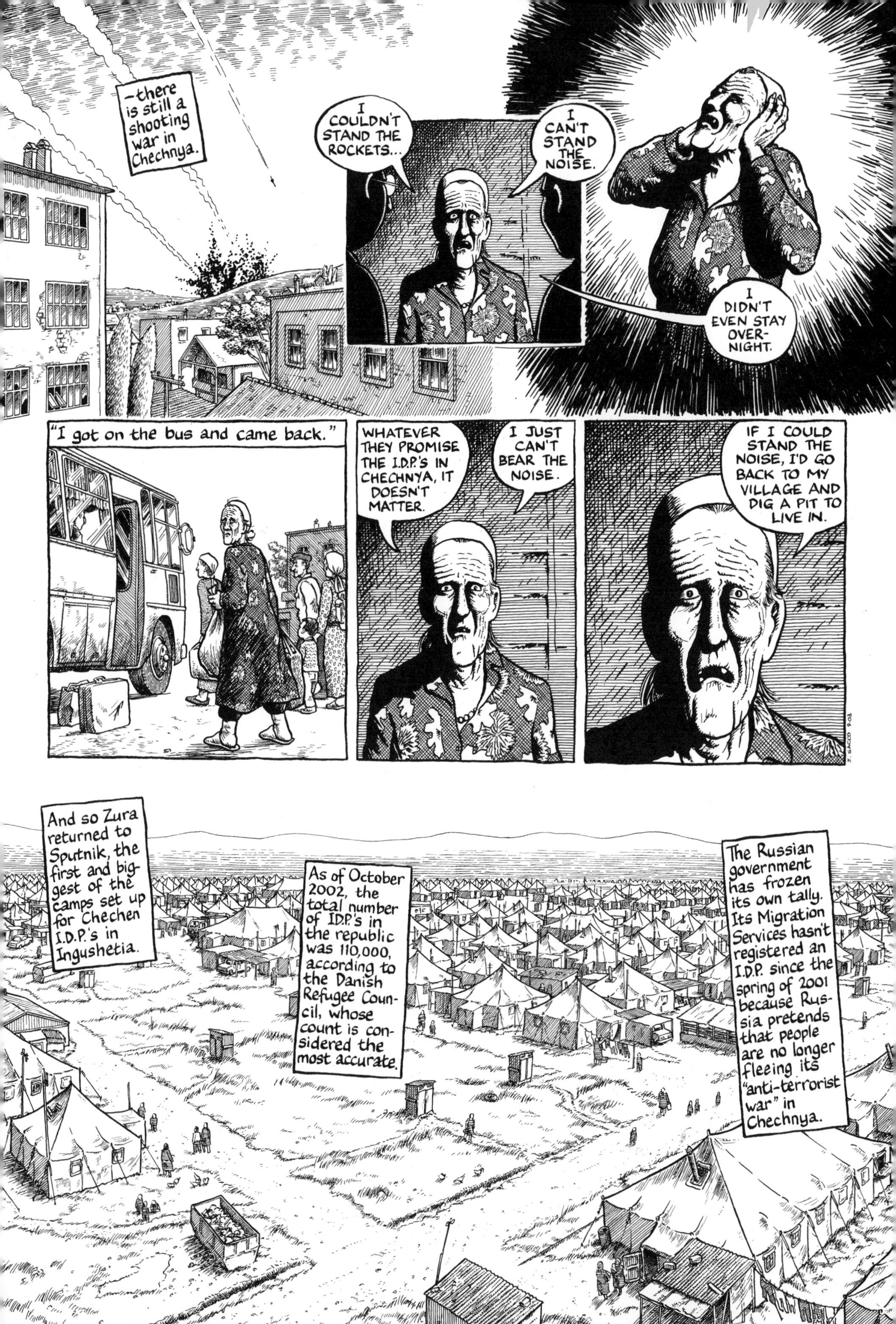
–there is still a shooting war in Chechnya.
I COULDN'T STAND THE ROCKETS...
I CAN'T STAND THE NOISE.
I DIDN'T EVEN STAY OVER-NIGHT.
"I got on the bus and came back."
WHATEVER THEY PROMISE THE I.D.P.'S IN CHECHNYA, IT DOESN'T MATTER.
I JUST CAN'T BEAR THE NOISE.
IF I COULD STAND THE NOISE, I'D GO BACK TO MY VILLAGE AND DIG A PIT TO LIVE IN.
J. SACCO 9-03
And so Zura returned to Sputnik, the first and biggest of the camps set up for Chechen I.D.P.'s in Ingushetia.
As of October 2002, the total number of I.D.P.'s in the republic was 110,000, according to the Danish Refugee Council, whose count is considered the most accurate.
The Russian government has frozen its own tally. Its Migration Services hasn't registered an I.D.P. since the spring of 2001 because Russia pretends that people are no longer fleeing its "anti-terrorist war" in Chechnya.

Chechnya's most recent anguish began in the early 1990's as the Soviet Union collapsed. The deep grievances of the Chechens against Moscow found radical expression in the person of Jokhar Dudayev, a former loyal Soviet general, who declared Chechnya's independence first thing after ascending to the presidency of the republic in 1991.

Chechnya, which is located in the North Caucasus, had a population of about 1.2 million, one quarter of whom were ethnic Russians. The Russians, who had enjoyed special privileges under the Soviets, made up the majority of the population of the capital Grozny.
Moscow
RUSSIAN FEDERATION
UKRAINE
CHECHNYA
TURKEY
SYRIA
IRAQ
IRAN
Certainly the Russians, but also many Chechens, did not want a total break with the Federation.

RUSSIAN FEDERATION
Caspian Sea
INGUSHETIA
Grozny
Nazran
CHECHNYA
DAGHESTAN
GEORGIA
0 50
MILES

Dudayev steered Chechnya—whose independence was never recognized by any country—out of Moscow's political sphere. Civic life deteriorated and poverty was widespread. Government workers went without their salaries.
The kidnap and ransom business, which had historical roots in Chechnya, reasserted itself.

Corrupt Chechens and Russian politicians took advantage of the lack of regulations, customs-free borders, and general chaos to enrich themselves.

Meanwhile, the disputes between Dudayev's supporters and his internal opposition turned deadly.
Dudayev had already dissolved Chechnya's parliament and constitutional court.

As Russia's media stoked long-held prejudices against the Chechens, the political will of Boris Yeltsin's government to negotiate with the problematic Dudayev ebbed.
Under increasing Russian threat, Chechens rallied to Dudayev.

J. SACCO 10.03

Using overwhelming force, including massive artillery barrages, the Russians devastated Chechen population centers.

J. SACCO 10.03

Shattered Grozny fell to badly bloodied Russian troops after a nearly three-month, block-by-block battle with Chechen fighters. Among the civilian dead—estimated as high as 27,000—were many of the city's ethnic Russians.

The Russian Interior Ministry set up "filtration camps"—supposedly to capture Chechen fighters—which became synonymous with beatings, torture, and murder, and whose chief victims were civilians.
Thousands were "filtered"; 1,500 are still missing.
Poorly trained and fed Russian conscripts were demoralized by a war they didn't understand. If they were wounded, even greviously, their government provided a pittance in compensation; if they were killed, their mothers might have to travel hundreds of miles to identify and retrieve their bodies.
Conscripts sometimes fell victim to robbings and beatings by their ostensible comrades-in-arms, the notorious Interior Ministry contract soldiers—the kontraktniki—often ex-criminals, who preyed mainly on Chechen civilians.
The state of the Russian armed forces was a prescription for robbery, rape, and murder in the areas "liberated" from the "terrorists."
J. SACCO 11.03
In August 1996, in a surprise offensive, Chechen separatists recaptured Grozny, dealing the Russians a stunning defeat.

A number of dramatic events in 1999 deepened the crisis. First, two warlords led a raid from Chechnya into the neighboring Russian republic of Daghestan, where they declared an independent Islamic territory. (Their "other" motives are the subject of some speculation.)

The raid precipitated the reemergence of the Moscow hawks. Yeltsin picked Vladimir Putin, the counterintelligence chief, to be Russia's prime minister.

With popular backing, Putin launched a second war on Chechnya in 1999. Federal forces took Grozny again after severe bombardments and house-to-house fighting and with seeming disregard for civilian losses.
Russian troops have managed to occupy most of Chechnya thereafter, but the separatists still operate and exact a toll.
Large bombs—including suicide bombs—have brought death not just to Russian soldiers and their local supporters, but also to innocent bystanders in places like Grozny's markets.
Those who remain in Chechnya must also contend with the danger of landmines, the imposition of curfews, and the certainty of power and water cuts.
And into this chaos, Russia pretends that it is perfectly safe for people like Zura to return and start their lives again.
J. SACCO 11.03

Or that it is safe for Raisa, who fled to Ingushetia after her husband was killed, and must now raise five children alone...
THIS BOY IS ONLY EIGHT YEARS OLD AND HE HAS HEART PROBLEMS.
HE FALLS UNCONSCIOUS WHEN HE SEES RUSSIAN SOLDIERS.
THE RUSSIANS COME AND TURN EVERYTHING UPSIDE-DOWN, AND THEY INSULT AND ABUSE PEOPLE.
THEY SHOUT AT WOMEN AND CHILDREN.
THEY TAKE EVERYTHING THEY WANT FROM THE HOUSES.
T.V.'S, CARPETS, CLOTHES.
IN ONE DAY THEY CAME FIVE TIMES.
THEY CAME MAYBE 40 TIMES ALL TOGETHER.
Or that it is safe for Zalva, who accompanies her sons daily through the many Russian checkpoints on the way to Grozny, where they study, and then back to Ingushetia, where they've taken refuge.
JUST LAST WEEK A RUSSIAN SOLDIER GRABBED THE SLEEVE OF MY 16 YEAR OLD AND WANTED TO TAKE HIM OUT OF THE CAR.
HE WET HIMSELF.
J. SACCO 11-03

But despite all the stories that filter in from Chechnya, despite what they know themselves, some I.D.P.'s still try to go back. Some feel their conditions in Ingushetia are too miserable to endure any longer.

Back in Sputnik camp, I meet Larisa and her sister Fatima, who tells me–

MY TENT WAS IN TERRIBLE CONDITIONS, ESPECIALLY WHEN IT RAINED.

I COULDN'T GET A NEW TENT.

SO WHEN EVERYONE PUT IN AN APPLICATION [FOR CHECHNYA], I PUT MINE IN.

EMERCOM, the Russian agency responsible for emergencies and natural disasters, promised her "a room with all the conveniences," and was so pleased when she agreed to move back that it sent a small truck to take her and her kids to Gudarmes, Chechnya.

But what is she doing here in Sputnik?
Is she moving back?
I WOULD COME BACK, BUT ANOTHER FAMILY HAS TAKEN OUR PLACE.
IF I WAS GIVEN ANOTHER TENT, I WOULD COME BACK WITH GREAT PLEAS-URE.
In fact, Fatima is here to pick up a hand-out from her brother and sister. They give her 1,000 to 1,500 rubles ($30 to $50) a month to make ends meet.
IF THEY HAD TOLD THE TRUTH, WE WOULD HAVE STAYED THOUGH IT'S DIFFICULT HERE.
Her sister Larisa tells me she lives here in a tent holding 36 people, where hanging sheets and blankets are the only partition between families.
WE'RE SO OVERCROWDED HERE THAT PEOPLE RUN INTO EACH OTHER.
Still-
I WANTED TO GO BACK TO CHECHNYA. I'M HAPPY MY HUSBAND HELD ME BACK.
J. SACCO 12·03

II. EVERY 50 YEARS

Asset lives in an abandoned milk factory called M.T.F. Karabulak.

Her family has three cows, which are out to pasture.

WE HAD CATTLE BEFORE THE FIRST WAR, BUT THEY WERE KILLED BY SOLDIERS.

AND THIS TIME WE BROUGHT THE CATTLE WITH US, NOT SO MUCH FOR US, BUT OUT OF PITY FOR THEM.

WE DIDN'T WANT THEM TO BE SHOT.

Asset knows full well that the recent wars are in a long series of historical disasters that have overtaken the Chechen people ever since the Russian empire pushed its way into the North Caucasus in the 1700's.

The rebellious Chechens—demonized as bandits by the Russians—were never fully subdued despite dozens of military expeditions to bring them to heel.

In the Soviet era, the Chechens resisted Stalin's agricultural collectivization. In one day in 1937 the Red Army rounded up and shot 14,000 Chechens.

But the worst was to come.

J. SACCO 12-03

*VAINAKH: THE NAME GIVEN TO THE CLOSELY RELATED CHECHEN AND INGUSH PEOPLE AS A WHOLE.

"The soldiers came with their rifles...
"and one soldier took me by the arm and threw me into a cart...
"The children were barefoot.
"We were taken to the collective farm, and as each family arrived, the men from that family were allowed to join them.
"Many families were separated. They couldn't find each other.
"The carts were set on fire. I saw for myself how the soldiers were shooting the horses.
"The Russians didn't explain anything. They just loaded us onto the train."

This was Stalin's final solution for the Chechens, whom he would later accuse of collaborating with the invading Nazis. His army had herded every Chechen and Ingush man, woman, and child onto trains— 12,000 carriages had been assembled for the task —and deported them en masse to Kazakhstan.

"It must have been a 17- or 18-day journey.

"At stops, young people ran for the food that was prepared at the stations. But the stops were short and too many people would be in line. And if the family didn't have plates, they didn't get food.

"When people had to go to the toilet they weren't allowed to go far from the carriage. When the train stopped they had to get off and do it right there.

J. SACCO 1·04

"Some people took wood from fences to make fires in the carriages.

"There was a small iron oven in the carriage so we could heat and make bread.

"I didn't have a blanket...[but] I was the favorite child. My parents and brothers tried to do everything so I wouldn't feel cold or hunger.

"I remember an old woman who didn't have children... and she stayed with our family.

J. SACCO 6.04

*KULAK: DEROGATORY TERM SOVIETS APPLIED TO PROSPEROUS PEASANTS.

What had been the republic of Chechen-Ingushetia ceased to exist. It was divided up and its parts transferred to neighboring Soviet republics. Russians and Daghestanis were settled in Chechen homes, and the Soviets systematically set out to destroy Chechnya's cultural heritage.

The Chechens were rehabilitated by Khrushchev in 1957 and allowed to return to their homeland, which was reconstituted.

But they were never compensated for their losses or for the brutality meted out against them.

The common experience of the deportations has left its indelible mark upon the Chechens.

Asset sometimes returns to her hometown in Chechnya to pick up her modest monthly pension if her son can't make the trip for her.

Sometimes she visits her old house.

I ask her to describe what she sees...

"I see a destroyed place," she tells me, "abandoned, overgrown with weeds."

ONE SHOULDN'T HAVE A FAMILY.

ONE SHOULD COMMIT SUICIDE.

ONE SHOULD THROW ONESELF OFF A CLIFF SO AS NOT TO SEE THIS MERCILESS WORLD.

EVERYTHING REPEATS AFTER A COURSE OF TIME, AND EVERY GENERATION GOES THROUGH THE SAME THING.

But what do you tell your children, Asset?

DON'T BUILD TWO-STORY HOUSES.

DON'T BUY TOO MANY THINGS.

YOU LOSE EVERYTHING AFTER SUCH HARD WORK.

IF THIS WAR DOESN'T COME TO AN END, WHERE SHALL WE GO?

THAT'S WHAT BOTHERS ME.

THIS BIG WORLD HAS BECOME LIKE A THIMBLE FOR US.

J. SACCO 10-04

III. THE CAMPS
Let's say you are a Chechen running from the war.
You get on a bus for Ingushetia's capital, Nazran, and you arrive some hours later with only the clothes on your back.
Where to then?
I ask Hazhan, who faced just such a proposition two weeks ago. She fled Chechnya with five children right after recovering from a bullet wound that had cut through her intestines in 13 places.
I WAS AT THE BUS STATION, AND I ASKED THE PEOPLE IF THEY KNEW A PLACE WHERE I COULD STAY THE NIGHT WITH MY CHILDREN.
And someone directed Hazhan to this automotive repair yard, Logovaz, in downtown Nazran, which has been partially given over to I.D.P.'s. It's a crowded facility with tents filling up the ground in front of the garages, but a few people made space for her inside a former storeroom.
Including her and her five children, about 15 people live here now, she says.
I DON'T WANT TO BE A BURDEN, AND THAT'S WHY I HAVE TO FIND A PLACE FOR MYSELF.
Hazhan has done what so many Chechens have had to do, namely figure out accommodation for themselves. There is no one to "meet and greet" the I.D.P.'s that trickle into Ingushetia, no central agency that directs them to this room or that tent.

Basically, new arrivals have one of three options:
they can fit themselves into a place like Logovaz, which is known in the parlance of the Non-Governmental Organizations (N.G.O.'s) as a "spontaneous settlement," basically an empty factory or facility already squatted by Chechens;

they can join one of the tent camps;

or, if they can afford to, they can rent a room or house for themselves.
Many opt to rent when they first arrive in Ingushetia, but they move to the squalid spontaneous settlements or overcrowded tent camps when their money runs out.

N.G.O.'s have struggled to provide the settlements and camps with basic facilities like toilets and baths and access to water, gas, and electricity.

I decide to check out living conditions by making a tour of as many I.D.P. sites as I can.
My sampling starts at the Plievo chicken farm.
J. SACCO 6-04

I meet Asya, who agrees to show me her basement room...

The place reeks so badly of mold that my head begins to spin.
Her mother has rheumatism, and her daughter has developed kidney problems, she says.
WHEN IT RAINS, THE CEILING LEAKS... FOOD IS DESTROYED BY THE DAMP.
WE'RE BUILDING ROOMS IN THE SHED TO MOVE THERE.

I walk over to inspect the shed she's talking about.

It doesn't smell quite so moldy in here, where the I.D.P.'s live in small, partitioned rooms...

They keep their stoves in the corridor to reduce the danger of asphyxiation or a room fire from leaking gas, according to the camp commandant. Gas surges make lighting the stoves for each use a risky proposition so the stoves are kept lit continuously.

At Plievo, people hang their food from the ceiling to keep it from the rats.
USA
SA
J. SACCO 10·04

For Yaha, mice and cockroaches are the least of her worries.

She lives in the sprawling ZhBi cement factory on the road from Nazran to Karabulak, which houses scores of I.D.P.'s.

Parts of the plant are still operating.

Trucks race up and down carrying loads from a gravel pit.

The dangers in this settlement abound. Yaha's eldest, Ilias, age 15, was killed when he touched an unprotected high-voltage cable.
WHENEVER I GO TO GET WATER I SEE THE PLACE WHERE MY SON DIED.
Her husband and a daughter were killed in Chechnya.
Yaha lives in this drafty former workshop with her five surviving children.
At the same settlement, some people motion me over to several large metal rings that open on an empty underground water reservoir.
One woman tells me that children playing here have fallen into the pit on a number of occasions.
She produces her four-year-old nephew.
He fell down there twice!
WERE YOU HURT?
NO I WASN'T!
Lucky kid! It's a 12-foot drop at least.
J. SACCO 7.04

Now, what about the tent camps?
Some of the biggest, like Sputnik, are situated in the middle of nowhere, close to the Chechen border.

At Sputnik, lines of toilets ring the tents or are set off a couple of dozen meters from the dusty roads.
Many of the old toilets, already full, have been abandoned where they are.
They are eyesores, like the tent camps themselves.

It is the tent camps—the most visible reminder that the war in Chechnya is not over—which most embarrass the Russian government. The Russians make bellicose statements about removing them, while promising the I.D.P.'s better facilities elsewhere.

Says Tamara, a resident of Iman camp:
THEY SAID THEY WOULD BRING BULLDOZERS AND TRACTORS TO SMASH ALL THE TENTS...
AND BRING POLICE TO BEAT PEOPLE WITH RUBBER STICKS.
J. SACCO 7.04

But why not leave if the authorities have offered you better places? It isn't exactly pleasant here...
Ahhh, Zulai explains to me, "pleasant" is relative.
WE CAME HERE AND FOR ALMOST TWO AND A HALF YEARS WE LIVED IN LEAKING TENTS.
WE HAD NO WOODEN FLOORS, NO GAS...
AND AT LAST, MORE OR LESS, WE HAVE GOOD CONDITIONS.
WE JUST RECEIVED A NEW TENT...
WE'VE RECEIVED OVENS AND STOVES.
THE SCHOOL STARTED WORKING.
AND NOW THEY WANT TO SEND PEOPLE TO OTHER PLACES BY FORCE?
I visit one of the places the Russians have promoted as an alternative to the tents—an abandoned distillery at Vozhesenovka, which now houses a few Chechen families.
Esita, who agreed to leave Iman camp with her widowed daughter and grandchildren, tells me—
I HAVE NO REAL COMPLAINTS.
Okay, she had to whitewash the walls herself, and there's still no gas, but—
COMPARED TO WHAT I'VE GONE THROUGH, I'M HAPPY IN THIS PLACE.
J. SACCO 7.04
A year ago, she says, after a hospital stay, "I came back and found out I had no place to live...
"I just found a clean spot.
"No tent."
The Chechen camp authorities in Iman collaborate with the Russians. In some cases they have removed the tents of I.D.P.'s who are temporarily absent, apparently hoping they will leave the camp all together.

But, Lyuba admits, she feared they would be moved from Iman anyway.

A REPRESENTATIVE OF THE MIGRATION SERVICES KEPT COMING AND SAYING THE TENTS WERE TO BE REMOVED.

TELL THE TRUTH.

THEY THREATENED TO BRING BULLDOZERS AND FLATTEN THAT PLACE.

J. SACCO 7.04

IV. ZARA
Zara lives in one of a series of disused cowsheds at a former milk factory in Altiyevo.

Did I say "disused"?
Actually, there's a pen at the back of Zara's shed—a dozen feet from where people live—that houses cattle brought over from Chechnya by I.D.P.'s.

The smell of dung in the corridor between the windowless cubicles overpowers the smell I'm used to in places like this—gas.
Watch your step though!
Exposed gas pipes lead off the main and cross your path.

Zara shows me into one of the two adjoining particle-board boxes where she makes her home with her seven children. Two to a bunk, I suppose.
IF YOU DON'T OPEN THE DOOR, IT'S TOO STUFFY HERE.
IF YOU OPEN IT, YOU GET THE SMELL OF THE COWS.
J. SACCO 8.04

It's stuffy all right, but as cheery as a room in a cowshed can get. She's hung up carpets on the wall.
THIS PLACE IS DAMP, AND THEY MAKE IT BETTER.
THEY MAKE IT COSY.
Zara bought these rooms for 4,000 rubles from the previous owner, who built them himself from donated material and charged her for his labor.

She's just paid another 3,000 on a room for her husband, who only escaped from Chechnya last month, and his two nephews, who were orphaned in the first war.
His name is Issa.
He is watchful but sits passively while Zara does the talking.

He has been tortured, she says.
Detained for six months.
Tortured.

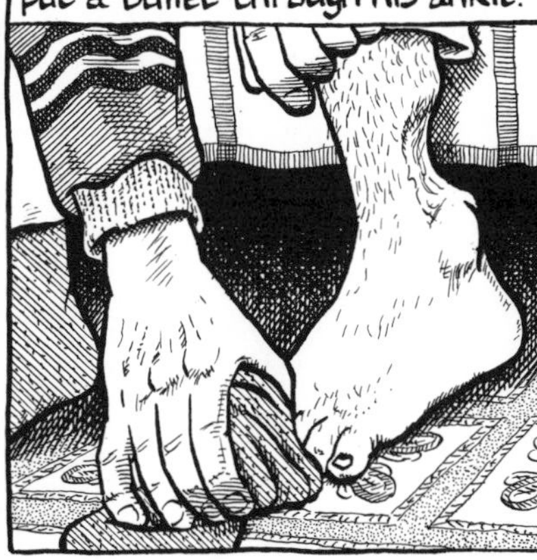
As if on cue, he hikes up his trouser leg. The Russians shot him, you see. He was sitting with his hands on his head and they put a bullet through his ankle.

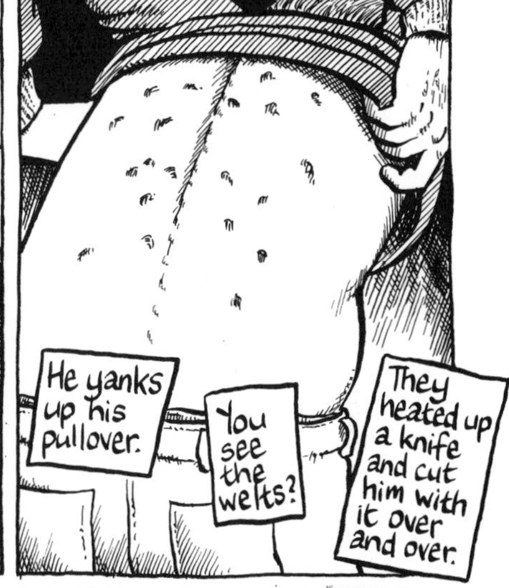
He yanks up his pullover.
You see the welts?
They heated up a knife and cut him with it over and over.

HE ALMOST WENT IN-SANE.
HE DIDN'T RECOGNIZE HIS OWN FAMILY WHEN HE WAS RELEASED.

HE BEAT THE CHIL-DREN.
HE BEAT OUR OWN DAUGHTER SO SEVERELY THAT SHE ALSO HAS MENTAL PROB-LEMS.

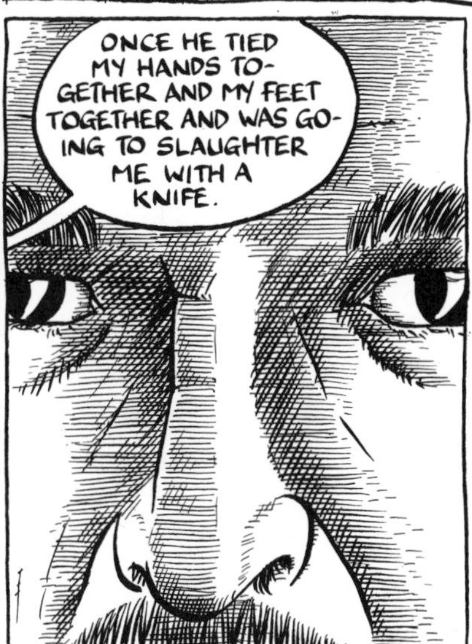
ONCE HE TIED MY HANDS TO-GETHER AND MY FEET TOGETHER AND WAS GO-ING TO SLAUGHTER ME WITH A KNIFE.
J. SACCO 8.04

HE'S BETTER NOW.
In the second war, Zara was wounded and fled Grozny with the children after their home was completely destroyed. Issa, whose passport and papers had been lost, remained behind. Without identification, he was unwilling to risk the journey to Ingushetia and another arrest by the Russians. He didn't even dare step out of his brother's house.

"Almost every week I would go to Chechnya to bring him food," Zara tells me. "I had to take him food from my family's humanitarian ration or he would have died of hunger.
"When I couldn't go for three months, I found him eating unground wheat and drinking sunflower oil."

She decided to chance getting him out. She paid a taxi driver 1,000 rubles—$33—to find a route around the many Russian checkpoints to Ingushetia.

And now he is here with them...
an invalid.

But if he cannot work, and if you are responsible for him, for his two nephews, and for your seven children, how do you make ends meet?
SOMETIMES I'M SURPRISED MYSELF.
BECAUSE GOD HELPS ME, I MANAGE.
Yes, yes, there's God...

J. SACCO 9-04

and there's humanitarian relief, too.

Relatives and a kind woman named Raisa helped when Zara didn't have a ruble to her name.

Someone else gave her two mattresses and a blanket for the children.

Now she works in the market, she says...

but it's hard.

EVERYTHING IS HARD.

IF MY CHILDREN ARE SICK, I CAN'T AFFORD TO TAKE THEM TO A DOCTOR.

I HAVE TO LET THEM GET OVER THEIR ILLNESS THEMSELVES.

I never know what to say to someone who thinks I have connections with important officials who can tend to her special case.

I think she means ten at night.
NO...
TEN IN THE MORN-ING.

Ten in the morning?
Are you kidding?
NO, AND THEN I WORK UNTIL NOON AT ANOTHER PLACE SELLING BIS-CUITS AND CAKE.
But that's a total of 17 hours!

HOW CAN YOU DO THAT? WHEN DO YOU SLEEP?
YESTERDAY I SLEPT ONLY TWO HOURS. IT'S JUST TOO NOISY.

SOMETIMES I FALL ASLEEP AT THE KIOSK, AND A CUSTOMER COMES AND WAKES ME.

Our con-versation is cut short 'cause here we are.
We drop Zara off.
She's thanking us.
J. SACCO 9.04

We've saved her a long walk.

V. GETTING BY

"I do the washing when the children are asleep," she says. "I'm lucky I have good neighbors who give me soap and detergent.

"The other women have given me some shoes for the children."

The most important thing her new roommates have done for Hazhan is help her get on the Danish Refugee Council list.

Of all the lists, this is the one that matters most.

Everyone on it is ensured a basic monthly ration of food—flour, oil, sugar, and iodized salt.

It's up to international aid agencies to tend to the basic needs of the I.D.P.'s.

The Russian government stopped providing soup and bread to the I.D.P.'s in 2001.

The international aid groups hand out building materials, tents, and necessities like stoves, but there is never enough to go around.
Hadet, who lives at the abandoned milk factory at Altiyevo, tells me-
RECENTLY AN AGENCY CAME AROUND DISTRIBUTING MATTRESSES, BUT WE WERE NOT ON THE LIST AND DIDN'T GET EVEN ONE.
Hadet, her husband, and their three grandchildren must share two single matresses between them.

What about these other possessions, these pans, these buckets?
THE THINGS WE HAVE ARE PRESENTS FROM OUR DAUGHTER.

Hadet must supplement whatever is given out.
When I meet her, she was getting ready to walk to nearby fields to collect small potatoes that Ingush farmers hadn't bothered to dig up.

Most I.D.P.'s try to earn money in some way or other. Hazhan, for example, has already sold her gold rings, earrings, and bracelets. One of her children now helps out by selling cassettes in the market while Hazhan washes floors.
I HAVE HIGHER EDUCATION...
I WAS AN ACCOUNTANT, A TECHNICAL INSTITUTE GRADUATE...
AND I'M FULL OF ENERGY.
I THINK I WILL OVERCOME THIS.

UNFORTUNATELY, MY HEALTH ISN'T GOOD.
J. SACCO 9.04

Malika, who lives in the Yandare spontaneous settlement, is luckier than most. Her husband has a job as a bricklayer, and she works plastering walls. Do they make enough?
IF WE HAD ENOUGH, MY CHILD WOULDN'T BE WEARING THIS TORN STOCKING.
Other I.D.P.'s — widows and their children, the elderly — rely on pensions to help them get by. Unfortunately, they have to collect them in their hometowns in wartorn Chechnya.
I ask Raisa, the widow with five kids whom you've met before, if she's afraid to return to her village to pick up the family's monthly pension, which totals 3,500 rubles ($115).
OF COURSE I'M AFRAID.
IT'S AN EIGHT-HOUR ROUNDTRIP, AND THERE ARE 17 CHECK-POINTS EACH WAY.
Back at the cement factory, Yaha tells me she goes to Grozny every month to collect 700 rubles — about $23 — for herself and for each of her children. How does she manage on that?
I HAVE TO CUT SOME-THING.
FOR EXAMPLE, I DON'T HAVE WIN-TER CLOTHES, AND THE CHILDREN DON'T HAVE SOCKS.
WHEN MY HUSBAND WAS ALIVE, WE HAD CATTLE, SHEEP.
WE ALWAYS HAD MEAT.
I WANT MY CHILDREN TO HAVE GOOD FOOD.
WHAT DID YOU EAT LAST NIGHT?
WATER-MELON AND BREAD.
J. SACCO 9.04

When I first met Hazhan, the new arrival at Logovaz, she said...
THE DOCTOR TOLD ME I'M LUCKY I RECOVERED FROM MY WOUND.
I SHOULD HAVE SPENT MORE TIME IN HOSPITAL, BUT I NEED TO MAKE MONEY FOR THE KIDS.
One or two days later I'm at Logovaz where I find some of Hazhan's children.
One kid runs off to fetch Hazhan, while another, not yet in her teens, tends to a baby and a younger brother.
The little boy is balling his head off!
He's inconsolable!
My guide tries to sweet talk him out of his tears, but the boy only cranks up the volume!
What a racket!
Thank God, here's Hazhan hurrying along to meet us.
I WAS AT THE DOCTOR BECAUSE I BURST SOME STITCHES CARRYING SOMETHING HEAVY.
She hikes up her only pull-over to show me the band-ages.
Looks like she's out of com-mission.
She won't be clean-ing floors again any-time soon.
J. SACCO 10-04

VI. ZAMANI

Zamani lives in a cowshed at the abandoned Nasir-Kort milk factory.

She isn't well.

She barely leaves her stuffy particle-board room, which is a bit more than six feet square and just over six feet high.

IF THE CHILDREN SUPPORT ME, I CAN GO OUT.

BUT USUALLY I GO JUST ON THE OTHER SIDE OF THE PARTITION.

On the other side of the partition is an unlit corridor that divides rows of similar box rooms made by I.D.P.'s from the same particle board or mud bricks.

Referring to the Russians, Zamani says...

"She was taken to hospital, but then the Russian troops closed the village. No one was allowed in or out for ten days.

"On the 11th day I was able to visit her.
"I told the doctor I'd come again the next day, but after I left the hospital she died."

Her other daughter, Samani, traveled from her home in Nagrovsky, elsewhere in the Russian Federation, to bring Zamani here. Samani then collected her children and moved in with her mother.
Wait!
You left your home in Nagrovsky for a cow-shed?
I'M USED TO DIFFICULTIES, AND INCONVENIENCES DO NOT SCARE ME.

MY HUSBAND REMAINED BECAUSE HERE HE WOULDN'T BE ABLE TO FIND A JOB.
AND HE DIDN'T WANT TO GET INVOLVED IN ALL THIS WAR STUFF.
She says she's happier here among her own people where her children can be raised with Chechen values.

"I don't like the behavior of the young boys and girls in Russia. They smoke, they drink, they could kiss, and this doesn't coincide with Chechen traditions and culture."
J. SACCO 10.04

But there was something else...

SINCE THE WAR BEGAN THE ATTITUDE OF THE RUSSIANS HAS CHANGED GREATLY TOWARD THE CHECHENS.

THE ATTITUDE HAS BECOME MORE AGGRESSIVE TOWARD THE SCHOOL CHILDREN.

OF COURSE THERE WERE GOOD PEOPLE THERE, TOO, BUT THE BAD ONES PREVAILED.

So now Samani lives here with her mother and four children.

They have two mattresses between them.

I BROUGHT NOTHING FROM HOME.

EVERYTHING WAS DESTROYED, BURNED.

IT WAS A BIG ROCKET.

BUT DID YOU AT LEAST BRING OUT A COAT?

I DIDN'T BRING A COAT.

I DON'T HAVE CLOTHES HERE.

ONLY WHAT PEOPLE GAVE ME... PEOPLE ALWAYS HELP EACH OTHER.

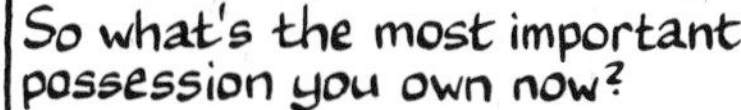

I CAN'T RECOVER FROM THE FEAR I HAD WHEN I HEARD THE PLANES. USUALLY, EVERY DAY, THE PLANES FLEW ABOVE THE HOUSE.

I CAN'T SLEEP SINCE MY DAUGHTER DIED. BUT, STILL, IT'S QUIETER HERE...

I'M SORRY I AM CRYING.

IT'S MUCH BETTER HERE THAN IN CHECHNYA.

I APOLOGIZE AGAIN FOR CRYING. MY DAUGHTER WAS VERY GOOD TO ME.

I change the subject. I ask about the deportation of 1944, which Zamani barely remembers.
THIS IS WORSE, MUCH WORSE.
NOW THE RUSSIAN TROOPS KILL PEOPLE WHILE THEY ARE DRIVING, WHILE THEY ARE TRYING TO FLEE THE WAR.
THEY CUT PEOPLE'S FLESH WHILE THEY ARE STILL ALIVE.
THEY DRIVE THEIR TANKS AND A.P.C.'S OVER THE WOUNDED.

I WANT TO SHOW YOU A PHOTOGRAPH OF MY DAUGHTER.
J. SACCO 10-04

Zamani takes a plastic bag from the wall.
It's not there.
MY GRANDCHILDREN HAVE HIDDEN IT AGAIN.
But why do you hide it?
BECAUSE WHEN SHE SEES IT, SHE CRIES.
Zamani sends her granddaughter to fetch the photo.
A minute later, here it is.
Just a photo.
A mother standing with her two daughters.
We leave Zamani with her daughters and make our way out of the cowshed.
J. SACCO 10·04

WHAT REFUGEES?

RUSSIA SWEEPS THE CHECHENS UNDER THE RUG

by Joe Sacco ©2002

Every so often, with a straight face, Russia's President Putin declares that the fight to keep Chechnya in the Russian Federation is won.

The bloody hostage crisis in a Moscow theater put the lie to that, as do the comments of Zara Ozdiyeva, and others like her, who continue to cross the border from Chechnya into the neighboring Russian republic of Ingushetia...

WE WERE ESCAPING DEATH.

WE LEFT OUR HOME AND EVERYTHING WE HAD THERE...

IN CHECHNYA WE HAD TO SLEEP UNDER THE BEDS BECAUSE OF THE BULLETS AND SHELLS.

My dear Zara! You are spoiling Putin's image as the man who brought order to the North Caucasus!

And so to bring reality in line with fantasy, Putin wants you and the 110,000 other "Internally Displaced Persons" (IDP's) either packed back to Chechnya — where Russia's brutalities against civilians are notorious in its "anti-terrorist war" — or scattered to less visible sites than this eyesore of a tent camp.

No camps means no refugees! No refugees means the situation is under control!

For months the word has filtered down that the clock is ticking for the Chechens who've found sanctuary in Ingushetia.

RUSSIAN FEDERATION

INGUSHETIA

NAZRAN

GROZNY

CHECHNYA

CASPIAN SEA

NAZRAN TO MOSCOW APPROX. 1000 MILES

0 MILES 50

GEORGIA

A 20-step plan signed in May by Ingush and pro-Russian Chechen representatives, under Russia's helpful direction, states plainly that the camps are to be removed and the IDP's sent back to Chechnya.

Haron Elzhurkayev, the commandant of a small refugee settlement in an abandoned chicken farm, describes a heated meeting between camp leaders and a Chechen politician who owed his allegiance to Moscow...

And in a tent camp called Iman an IDP named Tamara relates the threat made during a personal visit by Russia's First Deputy Head of Migration Services in September.

They didn't use force then, but are they about to use it now? Russian troops have surrounded the biggest tent camps in a move residents fear precedes forcible repatriation.
Officially, the Russian position is still that IDP's will only be moved "voluntarily."

But this fellow, Islam, a resident of Iman, isn't buying it. Ask him what "voluntarily" means. Other Chechen IDP's, collaborators with the Russians, carted off his tent while the rest of his family was away. He couldn't resist those goons alone, he says.
THEY SAID THEY WOULD SEND ME TO ANOTHER TENT, BUT THAT TENT WAS REMOVED ALSO.
And in this way the IDP's are encouraged to "voluntarily" go back to Chechnya or move to the abandoned Ingush factories the Russians claim are better than Iman camp. But Islam would rather live in this mud-brick room he's building.

Meanwhile, what is going on at Bart camp? Every day a truck comes and dumps gravel right where the IDP's live. The truck belongs to an Ingush company that leased the land to the Russian authorities to provide space for the spill-over of IDP's from Bart. But it seems the Russians haven't been paying the rent, according to Marietta Bokova, the camp's deputy commandant, and the company wants its land back.
In fact, Russia has all but reneged on its obligations to the IDP's. Gas and electricity are sometimes cut off for weeks because Russia will no longer pay the bill, and it has long stopped distributing a ration of soup and bread.
Four hundred people could be displaced here in Bart. But does that matter to Russia?
To hell with Rosa, whose tent is about to be swallowed up by the gravel!
THEY DON'T EVEN TELL THE IDP's TO GO OUT. THEY JUST DUMP THE GRAVEL.
THEY DON'T EVEN LEAVE SPACE FOR PEOPLE TO WALK.
But don't you get the message, Rosa? There is only one way to walk, and that is back to Chechnya. Help your president, Mr. Putin, declare victory—again!
J. SACCO 11-02

The Caucasus, Notes

"Chechen War, Chechen Women" was included in a series of books packaged together under the title *I Live Here* to benefit Amnesty International. The immensely good-hearted actress Mia Kirshner had assembled a diverse group of writers, artists, photographers, and designers to tackle human rights issues around the world that were receiving little attention at the time. She asked me to accompany her to Ingushetia to meet refugees from the war in neighboring Chechnya, and she paid for my flights, my accommodations, and our bodyguards. Bodyguards were a requirement for foreigners traveling in the area (to discourage kidnapping) and were probably there to report our movements to the authorities as well. We had three bodyguards each, and this amused me to no end. ("I'm sitting around with three personal bodyguards, sneering at journalists who've only hired two," I wrote in my journal.) But the entourage of bodyguards seemed to upset some of the traumatized Ingush refugees we approached, as I detail at the beginning of the story. I took to bringing only the most easygoing bodyguard with me into the camps and insisting the others wait in the car. Among the people who truly need protection in the Caucasus are the courageous staff members of Memorial, a local human rights organization, without whose help Mia and I could not have done our work. Memorial personnel have become targets of those who do not appreciate the exposure of ongoing human rights violations in the post-Soviet nations.

"What Refugees?" is an editorial, and it is perhaps the only occasion in which I tried to respond to a real-time situation immediately. It was completed for the *Boston Globe*'s Ideas section for deputy editor Jenny Schuessler within a few weeks of my leaving Ingushetia.

"Chechen War, Chechen Women" appeared in *I Live Here*, published by Pantheon Books, 2008.

"What Refugees?" appeared in the *Boston Globe*, November 17, 2002.

IRAQ

COMPLACENCY KILLS
by Joe Sacco ©2005
"When I'm on the road," says Sgt. Dance, commander of Mobile Assault Platoon (MAP) 4, explaining his policy toward Iraqi drivers here, "you're not on the road."
And so as we race to check on a report of some vehicles linking up in the middle of nowhere, the oncoming traffic had better get out of the way!
Lance Cpl. Janigo, binoculars pressed to his face, yells—
SINGLE!
—and Lance Cpl. Battles, the driver, flashes his lights until the startled Iraqi swerves off the road.
A single Iraqi in a car fits their profile of a suicide bomber, and our Humvee barely whizzes by that potential threat when two more cars come flying our way from under a bridge.
There's no time for Lance Cpl. Janigo to adjust his binoculars or for Lance Cpl. Battles to flash his lights!
Sgt. Dance screams—
GET 'EM OFF THE ROAD!
GET 'EM OFF THE ROAD!
—and Lance Cpl. Clark fires a burst across the front of the first car!
Both vehicles veer to a stop, and I catch a glimpse of a man with a moustache as we punch by.
J. SACCO 1-05

The primary mission of Sgt. Dance and the MAPs of the Weapons Company of the 1st Battalion, 23rd Marine Regiment is to keep the roads between Haditha and Hit open to U.S. convoys.

DAM
HADITHA
Euphrates
BAGHDADI
SAHILIYA
HIT
RAMADI
FALLUJA
BAGHDAD
BAQUBA
Tigris
RIVER
ROAD
0 25 50km

Their adversaries are insurgents whose chief weapons are roadside and vehicle-borne bombs and land mines. Twisted bits of car metal, charred patches of ground, and craters attest to the violence they've dished out to the Americans.

The Marines of the 1/23, who are nearly all Texan reservists, run most of their road patrols in this stretch of western Iraq from the functioning ten-story high Haditha Dam on the Euphrates River.

The stairwells reek of sulfur, but the Marines are otherwise smothered in home comforts: They enjoy a well-equipped weight room,

football on the chow hall's big-screen TV, and 24-hour internet connections to their wives and mothers.

I'm bunking on the fifth deck in a room full of officers where Lt. Crabtree, the battalion adjutant, projects a movie on the wall every night and dispenses snacks from an endless supply of pooled care packages.

The room's coffee aficionado is the commander of the engineering platoon, Capt. Kuniholm, and once I ask what motivated a married, liberal, business-owning Ph.D. student like himself to join the reserves knowing full well he would be sent to Iraq. A sense of duty, he answers.

Almost discordantly in this cocooned world of X-Boxes and Maxim magazines, a sign on the second deck reminds the Marines of the MAPs heading down to their Humvees that–

J. SACCO 1.05

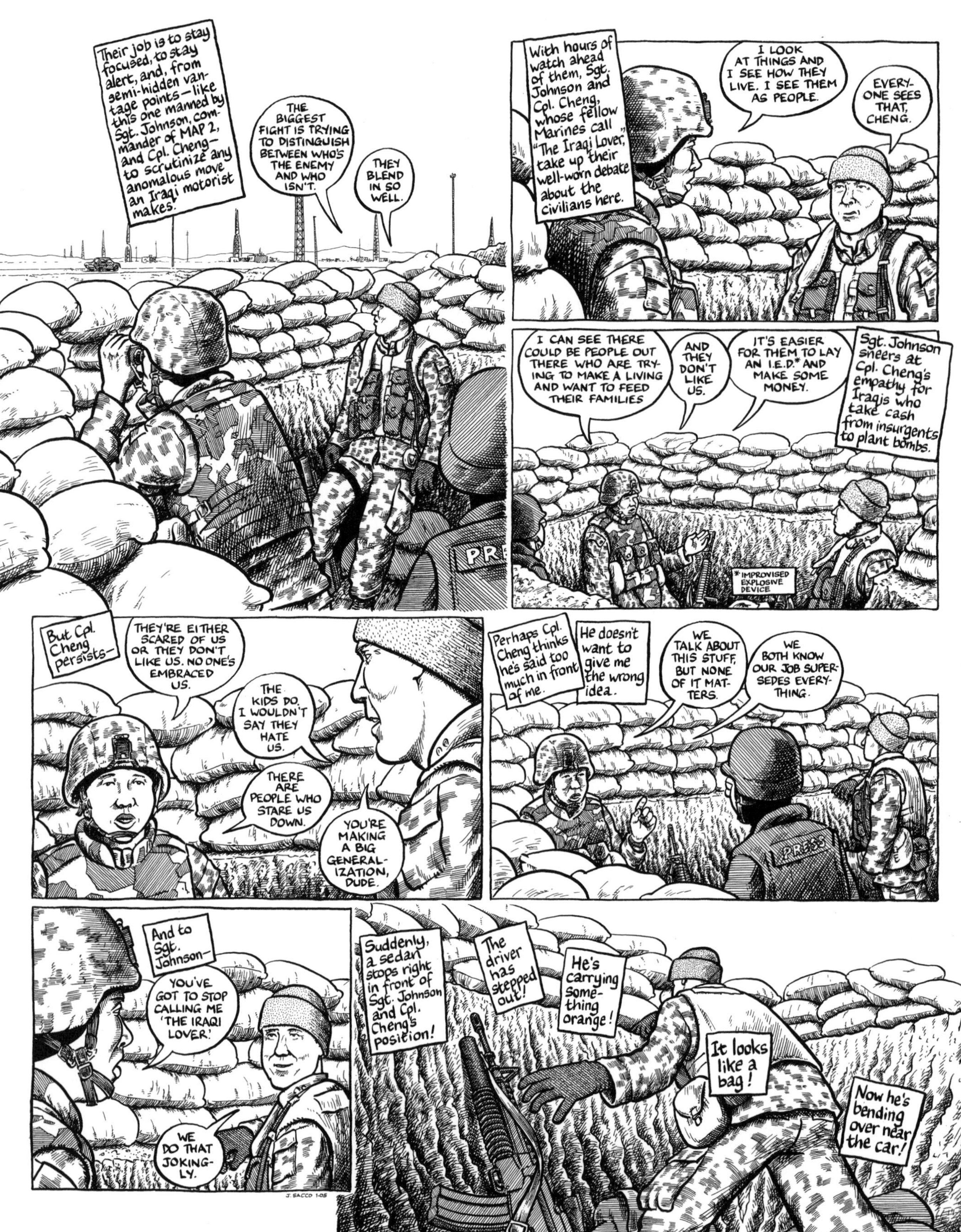
Their job is to stay focused, to stay alert, and, from semi-hidden vantage points—like this one manned by Sgt. Johnson, commander of MAP 2, and Cpl. Cheng—to scrutinize any anomalous move an Iraqi motorist makes.
THE BIGGEST FIGHT IS TRYING TO DISTINGUISH BETWEEN WHO'S THE ENEMY AND WHO ISN'T.
THEY BLEND IN SO WELL.
PRESS
With hours of watch ahead of them, Sgt. Johnson and Cpl. Cheng, whose fellow Marines call "The Iraqi Lover," take up their well-worn debate about the civilians here.
I LOOK AT THINGS AND I SEE HOW THEY LIVE. I SEE THEM AS PEOPLE.
EVERYONE SEES THAT, CHENG.
I CAN SEE THERE COULD BE PEOPLE OUT THERE WHO ARE TRYING TO MAKE A LIVING AND WANT TO FEED THEIR FAMILIES
AND THEY DON'T LIKE US.
IT'S EASIER FOR THEM TO LAY AN I.E.D.* AND MAKE SOME MONEY.
Sgt. Johnson sneers at Cpl. Cheng's empathy for Iraqis who take cash from insurgents to plant bombs.
*IMPROVISED EXPLOSIVE DEVICE
But Cpl. Cheng persists—
THEY'RE EITHER SCARED OF US OR THEY DON'T LIKE US. NO ONE'S EMBRACED US.
THE KIDS DO. I WOULDN'T SAY THEY HATE US.
THERE ARE PEOPLE WHO STARE US DOWN.
YOU'RE MAKING A BIG GENERALIZATION, DUDE.
Perhaps Cpl. Cheng thinks he's said too much in front of me.
He doesn't want to give me the wrong idea.
WE TALK ABOUT THIS STUFF, BUT NONE OF IT MATTERS.
WE BOTH KNOW OUR JOB SUPERSEDES EVERYTHING.
PRESS
And to Sgt. Johnson—
YOU'VE GOT TO STOP CALLING ME 'THE IRAQI LOVER.'
WE DO THAT JOKINGLY.
J. SACCO 1-08
Suddenly, a sedan stops right in front of Sgt. Johnson and Cpl. Cheng's position!
The driver has stepped out!
He's carrying something orange!
It looks like a bag!
Now he's bending over near the car!

Sgt. Johnson creeps toward the road keeping the Iraqi in his sights.
He wants a better view of what the driver is doing.
I take a look at the driver myself.
HE'S PRAYING.
Granted, he seems to be praying unusually fast...
Is the praying a ruse?
HE WAS LOOKING AROUND LIKE HE WAS SCOPING OUT THE AREA.
Minutes later, the driver leaves, but Cpl. Cheng's still suspicious.
The orange bag "could have been a prayer mat," he agrees—
—BUT I HAVEN'T SEEN TOO MANY PEOPLE GETTING OUT OF THEIR CARS TO PRAY.
MAYBE HE WAS CHECKING OUR REACTION, SEEING HOW LONG IT WOULD TAKE FOR THE HUMVEES TO GET OVER HERE.
MAYBE I'M OVER-ANALYZING.
And so ends another frustrating episode for the Marines of MAP 2, who would like nothing better than to capture or kill an insurgent in the act of planting a bomb.
One of their platoon-mates, Cpl. Kolda, was killed four weeks ago when an abandoned car he was investigating blew up.
He was evacuated in this open-bed Humvee, called a highback, commanded by Sgt. Cantu.
I'D LIKE TO THINK HE DIED RIGHT AWAY.
THAT WOULD MAKE ME FEEL BETTER.
WE GAVE HIM C.P.R., BUT I THINK HE WAS ALREADY GONE.
Two of Sgt. Cantu's crew bear the effects of near misses by suicide bombers.
Lance Cpl. Ledesma is slowly regaining his hearing after one blast;
driver Cpl. Heredia's ear was scarred by shrapnel from another.
J. SACCO 1.05

But even these veterans are lulled by the quiet of the last few weeks, and, on a hilltop buffeted by cold winds, they break the tedium of another 13-hour patrol with a hot dinner of canned ravioli and chicken soup.
Then...
in the distance...
a massive blast!
THAT THING SOUNDED LIKE A FUCKING S.V.B.I.E.D*! THAT THING WAS BIG!
GO! GO! GO!
* SUICIDE VEHICLE-BORNE IMPROVISED EXPLOSIVE DEVICE
Everyone's wound up like I haven't seen them before!
Everyone aims a weapon at the Iraqi cars, which pull over pronto!
We reach a group of Humvees from another mission.
A roadside bomb went off between two vehicles in an area the Marines I'm with had checked out in the morning.
One Marine, Lance Cpl. Knepper, has shrapnel in his right arm.
Lance Cpl. Knepper, accompanied by his platoon medic, Doc Perez, climbs into our high-back, which races for Haditha Dam escorted by the Humvees of MAP 2.
WHEN'S THIS MORPHINE GOING TO KICK IN?
As soon as the injured Marine is passed off to the Battalion Aid Station, Sgt. Johnson and Sgt. Cantu ask each other the same question: How did the insurgents place a bomb under so many Marine noses?
DIDN'T YOU SWEEP THAT AREA?
WE DID SWEEP THAT AREA!
I SWEPT IT!
J. SACCO 2-08

When Marines shoot innocent Iraqis, the battalion offers "salacia payments" of up to $2,500 to the victim or the victim's family to express "sympathy, not liability," according to Major Coakley, the unit's Staff Judge Advocate. In its five months in Iraq, the battalion has made "no more than ten" such payments for civilian deaths, mostly involving people in cars who inadvertently ran Marine roadblocks.

We reach the stopped car, a taxi.
The platoon's other Humvees join us and take up position.
No one's in the mood for games.
THEY'RE WAVING A WHITE FUCKING FLAG!

The Marines motion the Iraqis out of their vehicle. Sgt. Cantu and Lance Cpl. Ledesma, who has taken a crash course in Arabic, dismount and approach them.
The passengers turn out to be a family.
Their taxi has broken down.

We find another hilltop.
The crew begins to unwind.
One or two of them will catch some sleep.
But not Sgt. Cantu.
He's beating himself up about the bomb that went off earlier.
IT HAPPENED ON OUR WATCH.
WE WERE SUPPOSED TO SECURE THE AREA.
THERE'S ALWAYS MORE WE COULD HAVE DONE.

EVERYWHERE YOU LOOK YOU SEE 'COMPLACENCY KILLS.'
IT'S BULLSHIT—

—UNTIL IT HAPPENS.

A patrol or two later, I become impatient with the cat-and-mouse game in the desert.
Frankly, it seems we will never see a mouse...
and
if we don't
do I have a story?
So I join the Marines' Small Craft Company on one of its river sorties from the dam.
I'm hoping to find some real action out on the Euphrates.

Afterwards, section leader Sgt. Czerwinski tells me that the river company has just come off months of hard patrolling and fighting in the Falluja and Ramadi areas. This new assignment at Haditha Dam should be—

The next day, his unit is ambushed after landing on the river bank to investigate some small arms fire. Lance Cpl. Parrello, who piloted the boat I'd ridden on the day before, is killed. Three others are wounded, including Capt. Kuniholm, my coffee-drinking roommate at the dam, who had jumped on one of the boats on the spur of the moment.

Within hours, Capt. Kuniholm's 21 pairs of black socks, his four year old's drawings, and all his other items are packed up for shipment to his family in North Carolina.

He will not be coming back. His right arm has been severed below the elbow.

A short time later, I leave Haditha Dam on a convoy bound for the Al Asad air base.

WITHIN A MONTH OF MY LEAVING, THE MARINES OF 1/23 AND THEIR ATTACHED UNITS SUFFERED SEVEN MORE FATALITIES.

December 2004. On the Euphrates River, in Iraq's volatile Anbar province, on one of the top levels of the Haditha Dam, isolated from the reserve marines of the 1st Battalion of the 23rd Regiment, which is headquartered here, two U.S.

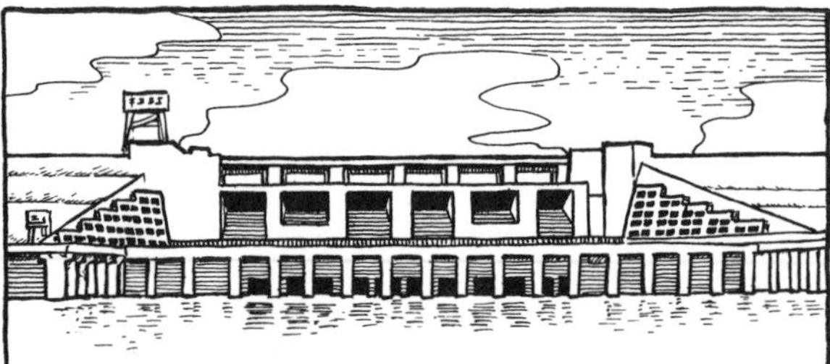

servicemen are tasked with shaping a motley group from the Iraqi National Guard (I.N.G.) into the sort of self-motivated, competent soldiers that can—in the words of President George W. Bush—"stand up" so that "we can stand down."

DOWN! UP!

by Joe Sacco ©2006

And if anyone is going to help Iraqis save Iraq, it is Sgt. Tim Weaver, but they won't be saving anything, he'll tell you, until they get small unit formations into their skulls.

Unfortunately, this afternoon's quiz confirms that this lot can't tell its "skirmish left" from its "echelon right."

And that makes Sgt. Weaver one disgusted fifth-generation marine.

EVERY-ONE THAT MISSED ONE—

STAND UP!

J. SACCO 8.06

Sgt. Weaver and his Navy colleague, Petty Officer 2nd Class Scott "Doc" Saba, have just three weeks to whip these guys into shape before they'll be expected to "accompany and assist" marines on patrol, and so the Iraqis had better learn a few basic commands—in English—'cause any mistake out there and a bunch of friendlies are gonna get killed.

Sgt. Weaver, 28, a heavy equipment service manager in his civilian life in Crosby, Texas, can't believe these guys. They'd gone over the formations "with little army men" again and again.

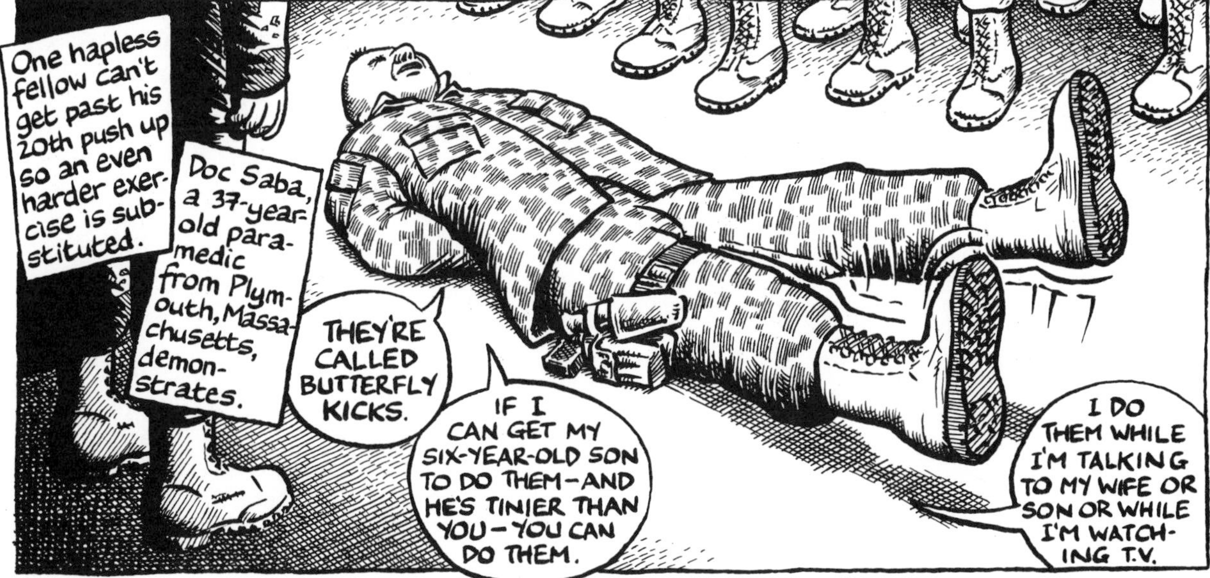

Finally, there is one guards-men left—
the one who cheated.
ON YOUR FACE!

DOWN! UP!
COME ON, BOOT! YOU CAN DO IT!
DOWN! UP!

GET OFF YOUR KNEES!
IF YOU HADN'T CHEATED, YOU WOULDN'T BE IN THIS PO-SITION!
THAT'S 30!
Twenty more to go!

ARE YOU GONNA CRY?
ARE YOU GONNA CRY LIKE A LITTLE BABY?
DOES IT HURT?
I BET YOU'RE NOT GOING TO CHEAT ANY-MORE, ARE YOU?

The Iraqi can't do another push up.
Okay!
He's sen-tenced to 25 leg lifts then!
GET 'EM UP! GET 'EM UP!

YOU STILL HAVE TO TAKE THE TEST OVER!
THAT'S WHAT YOU GET FOR CHEAT-ING!

J. SACCO 7.06

FOR THOSE OF YOU WHO ACED THE TEST, EXCELLENT JOB!
YOU HAVE TO PAY ATTENTION BECAUSE IF YOUR FIRE TEAM LEADER GETS KILLED IN COMBAT, YOU'RE GOING TO HAVE TO STEP UP AND TAKE OVER.
NEXT WEEK WE GET ON THE RIFLE RANGE.
YOU'VE GOT TO KNOW WHAT YOU'RE DOING OR SOLDIERS ARE GOING TO GET SHOT IN THE BACK.

While the men go over the answers to the quiz, Sgt. Weaver steps over to where I've been sitting taking notes.
SOME OF THEM ARE UNEDUCATED.
In fact, only five of the 14 can read and write.
THEY'RE BACKWOODS BOYS.
SOME OF THEM HAVE NO COMMON SENSE, NO COMPREHENSION SKILLS.

It's time to check the make-up test of the guardsman who cheated.
Oops!
He still got three wrong!
I TOLD YOU WE COULD DO IT THE EASY WAY AND LEARN, OR WE CAN DO IT THROUGH PAIN!

Sgt. Weaver orders the fellow into a stress position and tells him to hold it for ten minutes.
EVERY TIME YOU STAND OR TOUCH YOUR LEGS OR ANYTHING, WE'LL START THE TEN MINUTES AGAIN!

I'LL GET IN YOUR MIND!

Before too long, the guardsman squirms upright and drops his arms. He's made to start again. Minutes later he's babbling.
IF YOU WANT TO GO HOME TO MOMMA, I'LL CALL HER!

J. SACCO 7.06

Now it's Doc Saba's turn.
DON'T EVER WRITE ANSWERS ON YOUR HAND.
EVER.
THAT'S CHEATING.
CHEATING DISHONORS YOURSELF.
WHEN I SEE SGT. WEAVER, I FORGET EVERYTHING...

YOU NEED TO REMEMBER YOUR 'RIGHT' FROM YOUR 'LEFT.'

Sgt. Weaver, too, worries that they haven't got the basics down. He reviews hand signals they should know by now.
DIRECTION LEFT!
STOP FIRE!
ENEMY, 300 METERS!
They yell out the answers in English like happy school kids.

Sgt. Weaver promises real combat training after chow.
SO ALL OF YOU WHO ARE PISSED OFF AT ME, YOU CAN KICK MY ASS...

The Iraqis are given Meals Ready to Eat.
They pester Ahmed to translate what the packets and pouches contain.
THESE GUYS ARE IN MORE DANGER THAN WE ARE.
THERE'S MORE OF THEM GETTING KILLED OFF EVERY WEEK THAN AMERICANS AND COALITION FORCES.
WE GET THEM OUT OF THEIR ENVIRONMENT AND UP HERE 'CAUSE THERE'S NO TRIBAL CONNECTION AND THEY'LL BE ABLE TO FIGHT.
J. SACCO 7.06

In fact, none of these men, who were already in the I.N.G., knew they were in for this Marine boot camp stuff. One day they were locked in a room, and the next they were in vehicles heading for Haditha Dam. For security reasons they were not told where they were going; their loved ones still do not know they are here.
The idea is eventually to reunite them with their families at some location far from their home villages, thus snapping their old loyalties.

After their three-week course, Doc Saba tells me, they'll have a graduation ceremony where awards will be given to the best and the most-improved trainee.
WE'RE GETTING A PATCH DESIGNED FOR THEM, SOMETHING TO BE PROUD OF.
WITHOUT THAT PATCH, AS FAR AS WE'RE CONCERNED, YOU'RE NOT AN I.N.G. SOLDIER.
SABA
Doc Saba, who was attached to the scout snipers, and Sgt. Weaver, who was pulled from the battalion's motor transport unit, put this program together in just two weeks.
I LOVE DOING THIS SHIT.
I LOVE YELLING AT PEOPLE.

After lunch, Sgt. Weaver demonstrates the "basic warrior stance."
STEP! PLACE! STEP! PLACE!
It's time for the Iraqis to try.
BACK! BACK! BACK!
FORWARD! FORWARD! FORWARD!
J. SACCO 7.06

A few minutes later, the lesson disintegrates.
YOU'VE GOT SO MUCH ENERGY TO PLAY AROUND-?
EVERY-ONE, ON YOUR FACE!

DOWN!
UP!
DOWN!
UP!

I DIDN'T TELL YOU TO STAND AROUND AND BOX AND KISS AND TOUCH EACH OTHER'S BUTTS!
PLAY TIME IS OVER!
THIS SHIT COULD SAVE YOUR LIFE!

Sgt. Weaver tries organizing them again, but pretty soon they're cruising for another round of push ups.
DOWN! UP!
YOU'RE FUCKING THE GROUND!

But Sgt. Weaver isn't satisfied he's made his point.
He gets them into a new position and makes them hold it till they collapse.

Doc Saba tells them he can be just as ferocious, but—
—I'M JUST NOT IN A SHOUTING MOOD TODAY...
IF SGT. WEAVER AND I CAN'T TRUST YOU WITH PAYING ATTENTION AND LISTENING TO US, THEN THERE'S NO WAY WE'RE GOING TO PUT A WEAPON IN YOUR HANDS.
J. SACCO 6.06

THIS IS NO JOKING MATTER. WE ARE TRAINING YOU FOR A REASON.
YOU JOINED ON YOUR OWN INTO THE I.N.G. I DIDN'T FORCE YOU TO JOIN.
BEING A SOLDIER IS NOT EASY WORK.

Meanwhile, one guy still hasn't come to his feet. He's complaining about his hips. Not even Sgt. Weaver can shout him off the ground.

Doc Saba listens to the guardsman, but Sgt. Weaver's not having any of it.
LOOK AT THAT GUY. HE SAYS HE'S 28 BUT HE LOOKS 40.
HE SIMPLY HAS NEVER EXERCISED IN HIS LIFE, THAT'S WHY HIS MUSCLES ARE ACHING.
WE HAVE TO TEAR DOWN THE RECRUITS IN ORDER TO BUILD THEM UP.

WE'RE NOT TRYING TO KILL YOU...
I AM.

The next morning, before sunrise, while the guardsmen are assembled on top of the dam to take showers in relays of four, I ask to speak to the trainee who has seemed the most serious about his instruction.
His name is Qaid;
he is 24;
and he speaks English.

Unlike most of the others, he is well schooled. He has a degree in mathematics from the educational college in Ramadi.
But teaching jobs are dependent on connections and corruption, he says, while—
—YOU CAN GO TO ANY I.N.G. CAMP...AND GET HIRED JUST LIKE THAT.
J. SACCO 8.06

But now he is having second thoughts about the I.N.G.

I DIDN'T KNOW I WAS COMING TO HADITHA.

I DON'T WANT TO STAY IN THE GUARD.

FIRST THING, I LIKE THE CIVILIAN LIFE.

THE MILITARY LIFE NOW IN IRAQ IS UGLY.

THIRD, MOST OF THE OFFICERS ARE CORRUPT.

He says he intends to "quit" in a couple of months.

I HOPE IN THE FUTURE TO HAVE A SCHOLARSHIP TO GET TO ANY OTHER COUNTRY IN THE WORLD.

AND I WILL TRY TO GET ANOTHER CITIZENSHIP...

THEN I WILL BE HAPPY — BECAUSE I AM FINISHED WITH IRAQ.

RUN IN AND TELL OMER, IF HE CAN'T GET OUT OF THE SHOWER NOW, I'M GONNA CUT HIS DICK OFF!

I KNOW ARABIC, TOO:

'GET THE FUCK OVER HERE!'

THEY SEEM TO KNOW WHAT THAT MEANS.

J. SACCO 8.06

This morning, Sgt. Weaver is not in a pussyfooting mood.
YOU PUSH MY BUTTONS, I'M GOING TO FUCK YOU UP!

Even "good cop" Saba chimes in.
ANY OF YOU FUCK WITH MY SCHEDULE, I WILL RUN YOUR ASS TILL YOU PUKE, TILL YOU'RE CURLED UP LIKE A LITTLE BABY!

Today's class takes place on top of the dam. After some warm ups, the guardsmen are paired up to try the moves they learned yesterday. They seem enthusiastic about this kung fu stuff, about inflicting pain on their partners.
MAKE SURE YOU SPIN HIM!
DON'T FORCE HIM DOWN!
MAKE THAT ROTATION!
NOW YOU'RE GOING TO DO IT FASTER!
DO NOT HURT EACH OTHER!

Sgt. Weaver demonstrates a counter-move to a behind-the-back bear hug, how to rap an assailant's knuckles until his hold is loosened.
OR YOU JUST HIT HIM IN THE FUCKIN' NUTS.

While the guardsmen continue their training, I ask Doc Saba to assess his raw material.
ONLY ABOUT HALF THESE RECRUITS ARE WORTH SOMETHING.
In any case, he says, this course is too short. They need six or even eight weeks' training to be "minimally" ready to patrol with marines.
J. SACCO 8·06

Soon they'll be put on the firing range to test their proficiency on the A.K.47.

They'll be given only six rounds each, just in case–
Well, just in case they're bad guys bent on a killing spree.
AS FAR AS TRUST, WE DON'T KNOW NOTHING ABOUT THESE GUYS. IT NEVER FAILS THAT THE MUJAHADEEN PUT INSURGENTS AND SPIES AMONG THE RECRUITS.

Meanwhile, Sgt. Weaver has caught two Iraqis smoking cigarette butts and fibbing about where they got 'em.
YOU LIE TO ME AND I'LL SHOOT YOU!

And maybe he will, too!
He's drawn his pistol and loaded a clip!

I WILL SHOOT YOU IF YOU LIE TO ME ON PATROL!
YOUR LIES MIGHT COST MARINE LIVES!

After that drama ends without casualties, Sgt. Weaver lines up the guardsmen to test them individually on their hand-to-hand skills.
He barks out the maneuver he wants to see.
STRONG-SIDE WRIST LOCK!

Few of the Iraqis get the moves right.
I TOLD YOU TO FUCKING PAY ATTENTION!
YOU DIDN'T DO IT!

Sgt. Weaver starts throwing the guys who get the moves wrong.
J. SACCO 8.06

One of the younger trainees can't do a "leg sweep"...

so Sgt. Weaver does one for him.
Ouch!

MY HEAD! MY HEAD!
YOU'RE CRYING LIKE A FUCKING BABY!
YOU'RE A GROWN MAN, NOT A LITTLE BOY!

Doc Saba steps in. He thinks the fellow might actually be hurt.
MY HEAD!
HE'S PROBABLY NEVER BEEN IN A FIGHT IN HIS LIFE.
MY HEAD...
The kid sits out the rest of the lesson but he can't stop shaking.

By the way, everyone's shivering in the crisp December air.
ARE YOU ALL FUCKING COLD?
ON YOUR FACE!

DOWN!
UP!
DOWN!
UP!

A few minutes later, Sgt. Weaver is at wit's end. Only two of the 14 guardsmen perform the hand-to-hand drill to his satisfaction.
ALL RIGHT, DOC. I'M DONE.
IT'S KILLING ME.
J. SACCO 8.06

He thinks only five of the guards-men are worth his time.
THE REST OF THEM, THEY ARE KIDS.
THEY ARE NOT MEN.

THE ONES THAT ARE MEN, THEY ARE RETARD-ED.

Today's lesson sputters to an end, and it's time for a pep talk.
WHEN THE FUCKIN' MUJ JUMPS IN YOUR FACE, YOU'LL START PISSING AND SHITTING YOUR PANTS!
INSTEAD OF BEING AN I.N.G. SOLDIER, YOU'LL GO HOME TO MOMMA AND PUT HER TITTIE IN YOUR MOUTH AND START SUCKING!

IF I WAS YOU, I'D TAKE THAT TITTIE OUT OF MY MOUTH...
WEAVER
U.S. MARINES

GROW THE HELL UP...

AND GET THE JOB DONE!

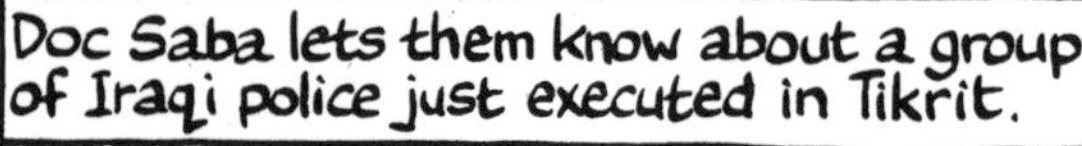
Doc Saba lets them know about a group of Iraqi police just executed in Tikrit.

THE MUJ PULLED 12 POLICE OUT OF THEIR POLICE STATION... THEY'RE ALL DEAD.
AFTER THEY'D DONE KILLING THE POLICE OFFI-CERS, THEY THREW A SATCHEL CHARGE IN THE POLICE STA-TION AND BLEW IT UP.

THE MUJAHADEEN DON'T GIVE A SHIT ABOUT YOU.
WE'RE TRY-ING TO TEACH YOU THE TRAIN-ING SO YOU CAN STAY ALIVE.

THE MUJ ARE REAL.
THE BULLETS ARE REAL.
AND IF YOU GET KILLED, THAT'S REAL.

J. SACCO 7.06

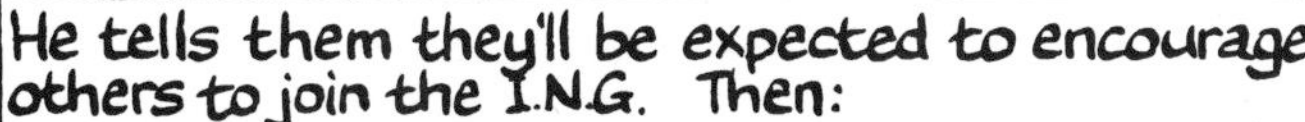
He tells them they'll be expected to encourage others to join the I.N.G. Then:

I spend a little time with a few guardsmen who are willing to talk to me.
They all seem to come from big families.
Most were out of work or underemployed when they joined the I.N.G., which pays a few hundred dollars per month—good money here.

They say they are proud to be guardsmen...
that they want to fight the insurgents...
and that they think the training they're undergoing is good.
I wonder if they are telling me what they think I want to hear. I wonder if they think I am going to report what they say to Sgt. Weaver or Petty Officer Second Class Saba.

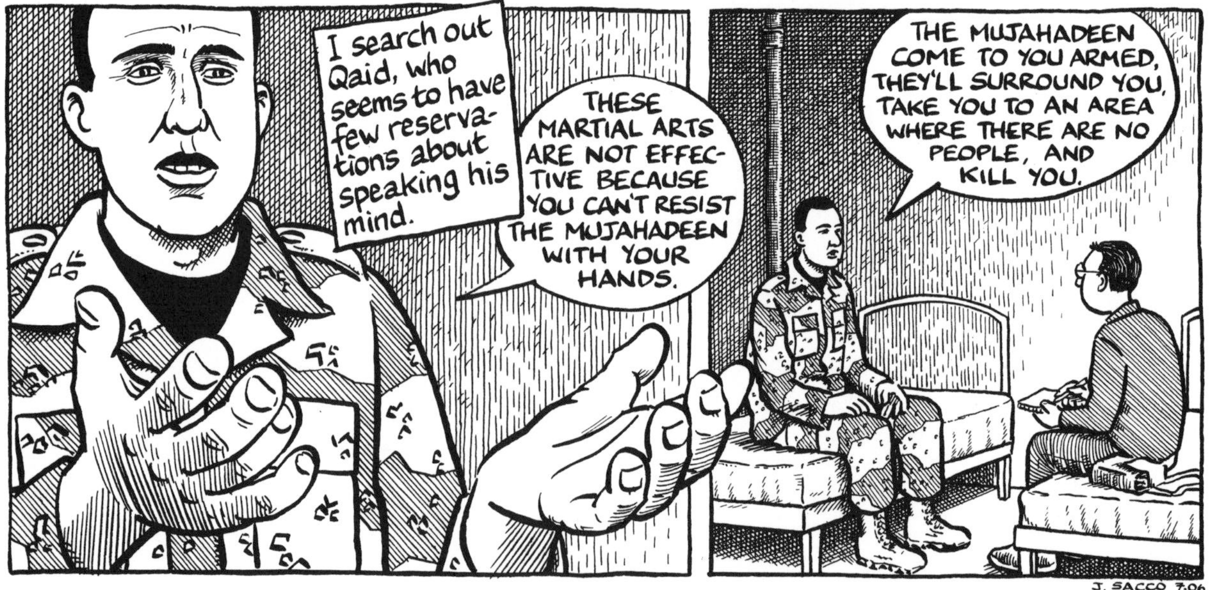
I search out Qaid, who seems to have few reservations about speaking his mind.
THESE MARTIAL ARTS ARE NOT EFFECTIVE BECAUSE YOU CAN'T RESIST THE MUJAHADEEN WITH YOUR HANDS.
THE MUJAHADEEN COME TO YOU ARMED, THEY'LL SURROUND YOU, TAKE YOU TO AN AREA WHERE THERE ARE NO PEOPLE, AND KILL YOU.
J. SACCO 7.06

Qaid tells me about people he's seen shot in the street, about friends killed since the war began.
Some student pals of his were spotted talking to U.S. troops and were then killed by the insurgents.
THEY THOUGHT THEY WERE WORKING FOR THE AMER-ICANS.
ALSO, FRIENDS GOT KILLED BY THE AMERICAN SIDE.
ONE WAS HIT BY A BUL-LET.
AND A FRIEND OF MINE IN FALLUJA — HE AND HIS FAMILY DIED FROM A ROCKET FROM AN AMERICAN PLANE.
He says the situ-ation is the same for "every young Iraqi man."
IF YOU WORK FOR THE AMERI-CANS, THE MU-JAHADEEN WILL KILL YOU;
IF YOU WORK FOR THE MUJAHA-DEEN, THE AMER-ICANS WILL KILL YOU;
AND IF YOU STAY HOME, YOU WON'T EARN ANY MONEY.
I leave Qaid and the other Iraqi guards-men resting in their room.
Sgt. Weaver will be coming through the door again soon e-nough, and they have thousands of push ups to go.
J. SACCO 8·06

YOU CAN RECOVER FROM PHYSICAL PAIN.
YOU CAN TAKE PAIN KILLERS AND MEDICATIONS.
BUT THE PSYCHOLOGICAL PAIN I SUFFER TILL NOW.
AND I CANNOT RECOVER, AND I CANNOT MOVE ON.
BECAUSE MY WHOLE LIFE CHANGED.
MY NATURE.
MY PERSONALITY.
AND I FEEL THAT I'M NOT THE FORMER SHERZAD.
I BECAME A DIFFERENT PERSON.
SOMETIMES I FEEL LIKE I'M CRAZY.
WHAT DO YOU THINK?
TRAUMA ON LOAN
I. 'JUST CONFESS'
by Joe Sacco ©2006
Thahe Sabbar and Sherzad Khalid have other things to worry about besides one last interview. Tomorrow they are supposed to fly back to Iraq through Dubai, and their transit visas haven't come through.
They are nervous, exhausted, filling their hotel room on Times Square with cigarette smoke.
But I have been lurking for three days—good-naturedly, patiently—and they feel they owe me.
They say as much.
And though I know it will wreck them to explain yet again how they—two businessmen; one an Arab, the other a Kurd; old friends; "soul mates," says Sherzad—came to be plaintiffs in a lawsuit against U.S. Defense Secretary Donald Rumsfeld, I'm not about to let them off the hook.
So with some reluctance, but graciously, they turn back the clock to that afternoon in July 2003 when they sat together in Thahe's office in Baghdad and heard the unmistakable squeaking of U.S. armored vehicles approaching.
What followed still bewilders them.
IF I COULD BE OF ANY HELP...
JUST GET INSIDE!
J. SACCO 12-05

According to the two men, American troops then entered the building "from all sides," including from the roof.
Sherzad: "They were yelling... and aiming their guns. And they started beating everybody."

Along with others in the building, they were cuffed, hooded, and driven away. It was nighttime when the vehicle stopped. "They kicked us off," according to Thahe.
"We fell on the ground... Our hands were still tied behind our backs, and we were still hooded."
Thahe's left shoulder was dislocated in the fall.

When their hoods were removed, they say they found themselves in one of Saddam Hussein's presidential palaces—standing in front of a cage of lions. The lions, evidently, once had been the personal property of Uday, one of Saddam's notorious sons.

One by one, the detainees were taken to the cage and, according to Sherzad, told to confess.
WHAT DO YOU WANT US TO CONFESS?
YOU DON'T KNOW WHY YOU'RE HERE? JUST CONFESS!

Thahe: "They opened the door... We went in, maybe a meter...

"But when the lions came running toward us, they pulled us outside...

"I lost consciousness. I was unconscious most of the time now. And the way they woke me up was by beating me..."

The men then were taken to a wall behind the cage.
THE OFFICER HAS DECIDED TO EXECUTE YOU BY SHOOTING. SO YOU BETTER CONFESS.
Sherzad: "And we didn't confess because we didn't know what they wanted us to say."
J. SACCO 12.05

* THEY ARE JOINED BY SIX OTHER PLAINTIFFS: FOUR AFGHANS AND TWO IRAQIS

So when their lawyers expressed misgivings about Thahe and Sherzad reopening their wounds for one last journalist—me!—when they hinted my interview might be cancelled, I wanted to snap back—

"Come on!

"You brought them here to reopen their wounds.

"No point worrying about their feelings now."

Yes, it's "the lion thing" that is raising eyebrows. Much else of what Thahe and Sherzad allege—the shackling in extreme temperatures, the electric shocks, the desecration of the Koran—might seem ho-hum to an American public that has long digested the enormities of Abu Ghraib.

And at his press conference, Mr. Rumsfeld called Thahe and Sherzad's lion story "farfetched" and referred to Al-Qaeda documents that—

—TRAIN PEOPLE, TERRORISTS, TO LIE ABOUT THEIR TREATMENT.

After perfunctory questions about weapons of mass destruction, Al-Qaeda, etc., the interrogator asked—

WHAT IS YOUR FAVORITE BREAKFAST?

WHAT IS YOUR FAVORITE SPORT?

WHAT TIME DO YOU GO TO SLEEP?

But then, does Sherzad know why he was subjected to "simulat[ed] anal rape" with a water bottle? Does Thahe know why "one or more soldiers in the presence of male and female soldiers inserted their fingers" into his anus?

I've quoted Thahe's and Sherzad's sexual assault allegations from the lawsuit. Their attorneys ask me not to bring up the subject with the men. When CNN broke that ground rule and badgered Thahe about his ordeal, he was retraumatized, I'm told.

*SADDAM HUSSEIN WAS STILL IN HIDING WHEN THIS INTERROGATION TOOK PLACE

IV. 'I HAVE NO DESIRE TO TELL A SAD STORY'
In the morning, an interview with 'Time' magazine; in the afternoon, a meeting with earnest Senate staffers who promise to relay Thahe and Sherzad's story to their bosses.
And now one of the attorneys suggests a quick get-together with her colleagues in an office nearby.
IT'S UP TO YOU.

But Thahe is only being diplomatic. He boards the van rented for the day's activities and waits for his handlers to follow.
WE WANT TO GO SEE THE WHITE HOUSE.
The lawyers are sensitive to the moods of their clients. The rest of the day will be given over to sight-seeing.

For an hour or two, Thahe and Sherzad smile in front of America's monuments to liberty.

But the cell phones are ringing again.
A senator has agreed to meet with Thahe and Sherzad personally.
When?
Now!
Thahe is almost despondent.
He has to remind himself why he's here.
WE DIDN'T COME AS TOURISTS.

Sherzad, on the other hand, won't have it.
AFTER SEEING THIS BEAUTIFUL VIEW, I HAVE NO DESIRE TO TELL A SAD STORY.
The attorneys turn down the senator. And they tell Thahe and Sherzad they will get to see the White House in the morning.

V. THE AIRPORT
AT THE AIRPORT, THERE WERE 75 TO 150 DETAINEES IN EACH TENT.

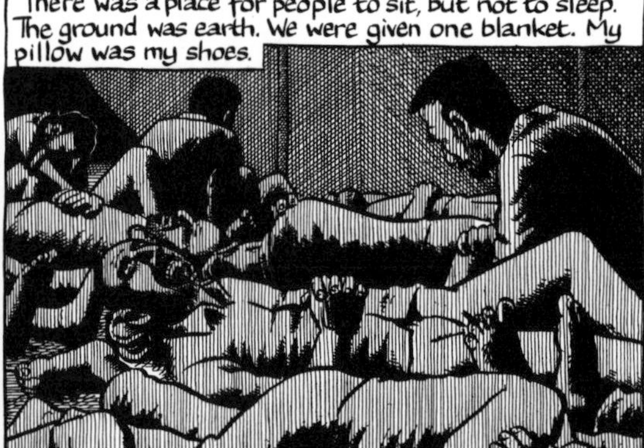
"There was a place for people to sit, but not to sleep. The ground was earth. We were given one blanket. My pillow was my shoes.

"I had a beard. I had long hair just like a beast.
J. SACCO 12-05

"Each tent had its own guard... The guard would bring a folding chair... and he'd sit with his water, and he had a carton of cigarettes, and he smoked as much as he wanted.
"We were allowed two cigarettes a day.
"One time, a very ugly person came.
I'M NOT GOING TO GIVE YOU YOUR CIGARETTES.
I'M GOING TO THROW A CIGARETTE, AND IF YOU CATCH IT IN YOUR MOUTH YOU CAN HAVE IT.
IF IT FALLS ON THE GROUND, YOU DON'T GET IT.
"The soldiers saw this funny situation, and they were coming over.
"One of the detainees was in front, and his actions were like a dog's.
"The soldier was faking as if he would throw the cigarette this way or that way.
"The soldiers were laughing. They gave him a lot of cigarettes...
"It was my turn. I told him in very basic English:
I WANT TWO CIGARETTES ONLY, PLEASE.
I DON'T WANT TO DO THAT.
"He opened the wire and came in... He beat me and he cursed me."
U.S. ARMY
VI. THE WHITE HOUSE
There's a train to catch back to New York, but a promise is a promise, and in the morning Thahe and Sherzad are taken to see the White House.
J. SACCO 12-05
And there they find a lone protester in a painfully familiar pose.
BAN ALL TORTURE NOW

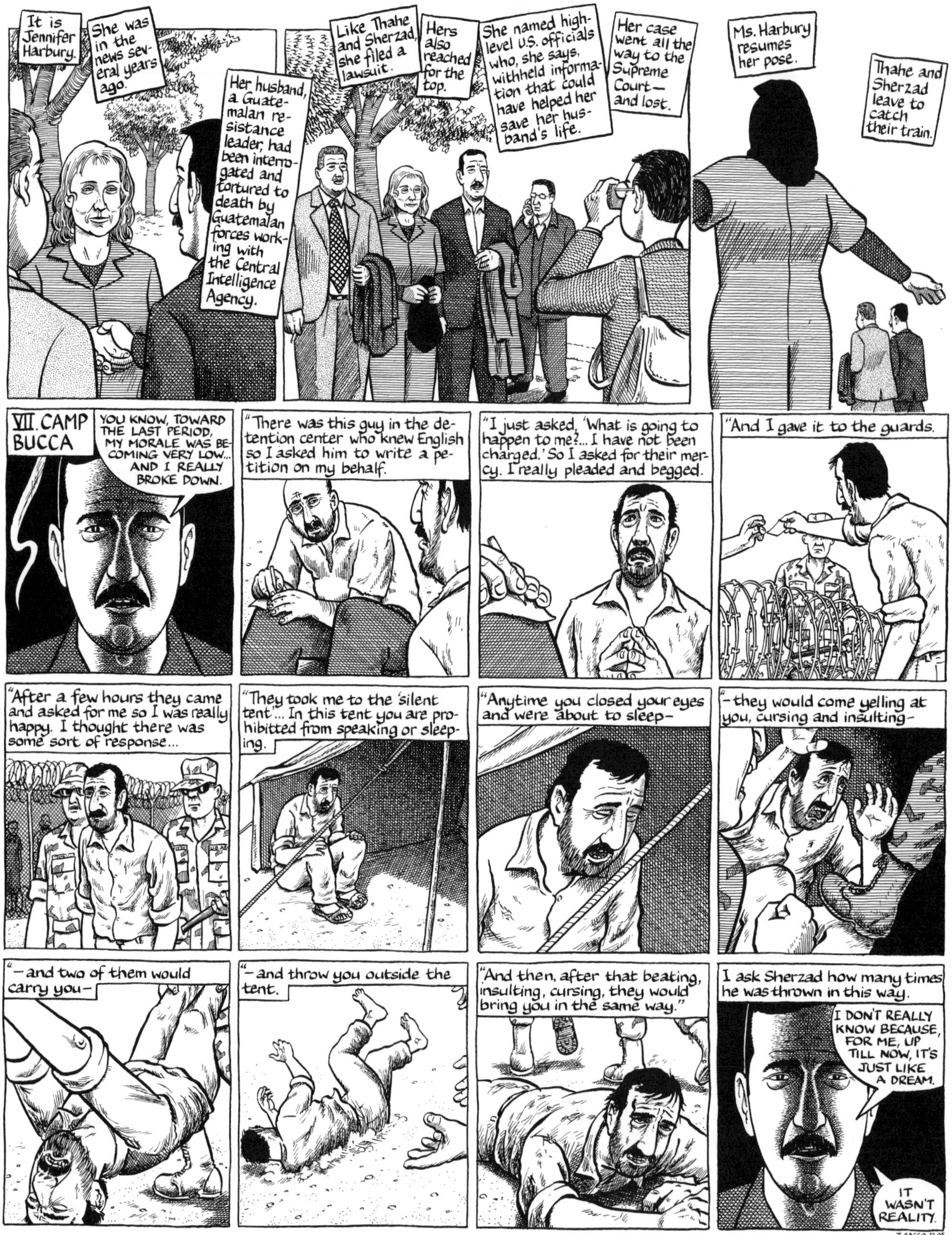

It is Jennifer Harbury.

She was in the news several years ago.

Her husband, a Guatemalan resistance leader, had been interrogated and tortured to death by Guatemalan forces working with the Central Intelligence Agency.

Like Thahe and Sherzad, she filed a lawsuit.

Hers also reached for the top.

She named high-level U.S. officials who, she says, withheld information that could have helped her save her husband's life.

Her case went all the way to the Supreme Court—and lost.

Ms. Harbury resumes her pose.

Thahe and Sherzad leave to catch their train.

VII. CAMP BUCCA

YOU KNOW, TOWARD THE LAST PERIOD, MY MORALE WAS BECOMING VERY LOW... AND I REALLY BROKE DOWN.

"There was this guy in the detention center who knew English so I asked him to write a petition on my behalf.

"I just asked, 'What is going to happen to me?... I have not been charged.' So I asked for their mercy. I really pleaded and begged.

"And I gave it to the guards.

"After a few hours they came and asked for me so I was really happy. I thought there was some sort of response...

"They took me to the 'silent tent'... In this tent you are prohibitted from speaking or sleeping.

"Anytime you closed your eyes and were about to sleep—

—they would come yelling at you, cursing and insulting—

"—and two of them would carry you—

"—and throw you outside the tent.

"And then, after that beating, insulting, cursing, they would bring you in the same way."

I ask Sherzad how many times he was thrown in this way.

VIII. RELEASE
Honestly, I've been gentle.
I haven't pushed.
I've jumped over whole allegations, entire beatings and humiliations.
I've curbed my enthusiasm for detail.
Yet even without the hints from the attorney monitoring our conversation, it's clear to me that Thahe has had enough.
CONTINUE WITH ME BECAUSE I'M STRONGER THAN HE IS.

So I go on with Sherzad for a few minutes more, but I know it's time to leave.
Because after awhile, in certain situations, a journalist in a room begins to smell; even he notices.

Still– I have one more question. Just one more and I'm going.
How were you released?
YOU KNOW, THE RELEASE IS RANDOM, JUST LIKE THE ARREST.

"Once you're released, you don't believe it. You look behind you because you're so scared that they're going to jump you and arrest you again.

"And I did not believe that I was released until I arrived at my house and saw my children.

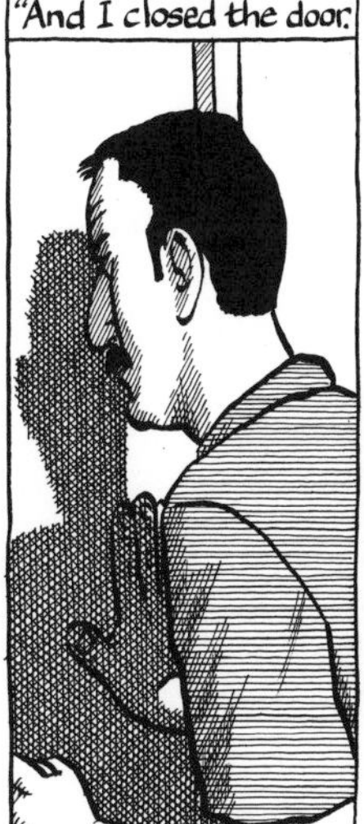
"And I closed the door.

"And I asked my brother to bring me a lock so I could lock the door from the inside.

"And they were laughing at me."

I pack my pen and notebook and tape recorder.
I get up to go.

I tell Thahe and Sherzad that I was honored to meet them.
I thank them.
I wish them a good journey back to Iraq.

And, once again, they are released.
J. SACCO 12-05

Iraq, Notes

I've heard much criticism of embedded journalism, including by people whose opinions I respect, and though I was personally opposed to the invasion of Iraq, I thought it would be worth my while to see things from the standpoint of those at the tip of the spear of the American imperial project. Of course a journalist begins to see things from the perspective of a marine when one is on patrol with marines, but to me that is the point. Ultimately combat troops are narrowly focused on the matter at hand, and generally they are more interested in taking care of each other than accomplishing anything more patriotic sounding. In that respect, almost all combat stories are the same, and I imagine "Complacency Kills" could just as well have been set during the wars in Vietnam or Korea. From that perspective, I don't think my story added anything new to the immense literature of "men at war," but what journalist doesn't want to see everything firsthand? The *Guardian* staff provided me with generous logistical support and didn't interfere editorially at all; the marines treated me with respect and kindness. I thank them all.

"Down! Up!" is a better story because it gets to the heart of the above-mentioned imperial project: the disconnect between what the results-oriented American overseers want and what the bewildered and traumatized locals are able or willing to do. Aside from a translator or two, the national guardsmen were the only Iraqis I spoke to while I was in the country. To me, they were civilians who needed a livelihood who had put on a uniform; I felt deeply sorry for them. I wrote the story as it played out in front of me. I was wary of working again for *Harper's*, but Roger Hodge, the new editor, made my second experience with the magazine a positive one.

Reporting for "Trauma on Loan," the story of Thahe Sabbar and Sherzad Khalid, was a very frustrating experience. I spent two or three days traveling with them to let them get comfortable with me before our formal interview. Consequently, when one of them told me he was going to tell me something he hadn't told other journalists, I thought I'd earned his confidence. The human rights attorney present immediately stopped him. She obviously had his interests in mind, but I resented the interference. Even when advocates and journalists share the same values they might not necessarily have the same goals. A journalist wants to know everything and insists on his own discrimination whether and how to present loaded material.

"Complacency Kills" appeared in the *Guardian Weekend*, February 26, 2005.

"Down! Up!" appeared in *Harper's Magazine*, April 2007.

"Trauma on Loan" appeared in the *Guardian Weekend*, January 21, 2006.

MIGRATION

Globalization!

Italian and French vessels snag bluefins in huge nets and then transfer them to Maltese fish farmers who keep the tuna captive until the day they're harvested, packed, and flown—still fresh—to Japan.

And so what begins in the Mediterranean Sea ends with happy burps in Tokyo's restaurants.

THE UNWANTED

by Joe Sacco ©2009

But here, off the coast of Malta, the fishermen harpooning and gutting the day's quota bristle at the mention of a darker feather in globalization's cap, the 12,500 mostly Sub-Saharan Africans desperate to reach Europe who have washed up on the island's shore.*

*AS OF AUG. 2009

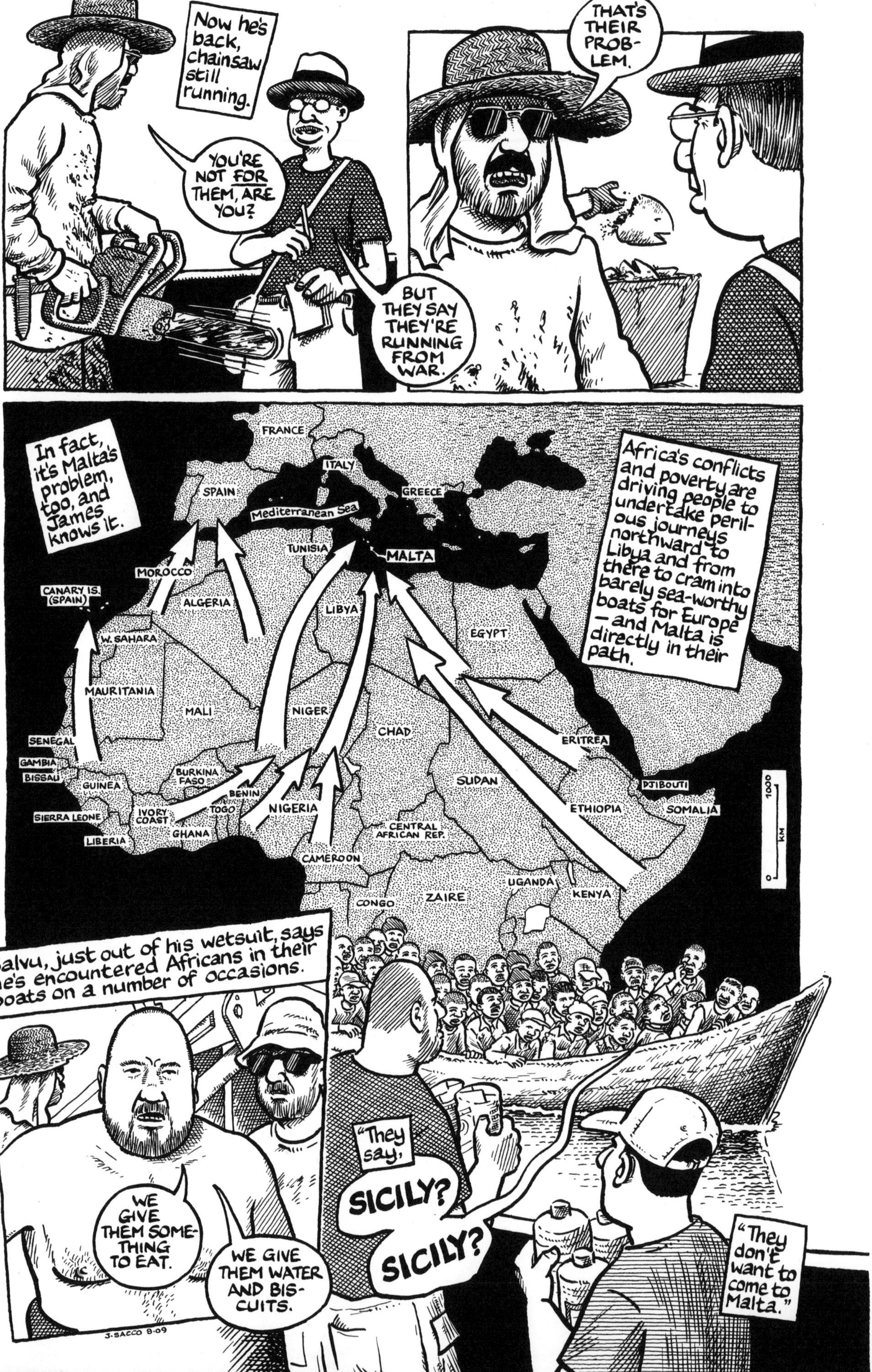

In fact, it's Malta's problem, too, and James knows it.

Africa's conflicts and poverty are driving people to undertake perilous journeys northward to Libya and from there to cram into barely sea-worthy boats for Europe — and Malta is directly in their path.

FRANCE
ITALY
SPAIN
GREECE
Mediterranean Sea
TUNISIA
MALTA
MOROCCO
CANARY IS. (SPAIN)
ALGERIA
LIBYA
W. SAHARA
EGYPT
MAURITANIA
MALI
NIGER
CHAD
SENEGAL
ERITREA
GAMBIA
BISSAU
GUINEA
BURKINA FASO
SUDAN
DJIBOUTI
BENIN
SIERRA LEONE
IVORY COAST
TOGO
NIGERIA
ETHIOPIA
SOMALIA
LIBERIA
GHANA
CENTRAL AFRICAN REP.
CAMEROON
UGANDA
CONGO
ZAIRE
KENYA
0 KM 1000

Salvu, just out of his wetsuit, says he's encountered Africans in their boats on a number of occasions.

WE GIVE THEM SOME-THING TO EAT.
WE GIVE THEM WATER AND BIS-CUITS.
"They say,
SICILY?
SICILY?
"They don't want to come to Malta."

J. SACCO 8-09

And the Maltese don't particularly want them to reach Malta either.
In one notorious incident, African migrants held on to a tuna net for two days after their boat sank while the Maltese fishermen towing the net refused to take them onboard.
Nor would they take them ashore.
The owner of the Maltese vessel didn't want to delay bringing in his catch.
It was left to the Italian navy to rescue the migrants.
But the Maltese cannot always avoid the issue, and they have become the unhappy hosts of many of those rescued at sea or desperate, after losing their way, for any shore.
IT'S NOT THAT THE MALTESE DON'T WANT TO HELP.
BUT WE'RE TOO SMALL FOR THE NUMBER WE HAVE.
WHERE ARE THEY GOING TO STAY?
IMAGINE IF THEY KEEP COMING.
The Maltese archipelago is indeed tiny, a total of 122 square miles...
0 2 4 6 8 10
MILES
MALTA
and with 400,000 residents it is one of the world's most densely populated places.
ST. PAUL'S BAY
SLIEMA
VALLETTA
ST. ANTON GARDENS
MARSA
TA'KANDJA
SAFI
BIRZEBBUGA
HAL FAR
ONLY SITES MENTIONED IN THIS STORY ARE LABELED
In 2001, looking ahead to a potential influx of what are now termed "irregular immigrants," Malta opened a facility to hold 80 people.
The next year 1,600 Africans landed.
The numbers kept rising.

In a single one-year period spanning 2008-09, 3,500 Africans arrived.

According to Darrell Pace, a government communications coordinator, that would be the equivalent, proportionally, of more than half a million immigrants landing in Italy.

ITALY CAN ABSORB THE NUMBERS; WE JUST CAN'T.

But it doesn't take an extrapolating official to tell you that Malta is experiencing a startling demographic shift.

Black faces are everywhere...

in the streets...

on buses...

behind kiosks...

And the Maltese don't like it one bit.

J. SACCO 9.01

There is a story going around that has gained traction in Malta. I heard it four times.

An African tells a Maltese policeman, "Keep the boats because one day you'll be on them."

But no one sent the Africans—the vast majority of whom are single Muslim men—an invitation to Malta, a Catholic and, until recently, homogeneous country.

When African immigrants arrive here, they are welcomed by detention for up to a year and a half (we'll get to that later) before being released to open centers, where they can come and go as they please.

Some of these facilities are in the heart of Maltese communities.

One of the largest is in a disused trade school in Marsa, a working-class town of 6,000.

J. SACCO 9.09

Its five-time mayor, Francis Debono, describes Marsa as a "quiet place" without tension before the government unilaterally decided to put an open center here.
I REACTED NEGATIVELY BECAUSE THERE WAS NO CONSULTATION WITH THE [TOWN] COUNCIL OR THE RESIDENTS.
He drives me by the Marsa Open Center one evening.
It's a social hub for Africans from all over the island, and though its official population is about 700, he estimates that up to 2,500 flop here at times.
WHEN YOU COME TO THIS AREA, YOU FORGET YOU ARE IN MALTA.
Can I imagine a woman passing this way? he asks.
At a nearby park, Debono shows me the empty beer cans and other litter he says the immigrants leave behind.
They get drunk and fight amongst themselves, he says, and the Maltese community isn't used to such behavior.
He motions to a group of African men drinking under a bridge.
IF THEY HAVE TO GO TO THE TOILET, THEY JUST DO IT, EVEN IN FRONT OF THE CHILDREN.
J. SACCO 9.09

Debono takes me to Prince Albert Street, where a row of houses is sandwiched between the open center and Marsa's industrial zone.
We pull over to speak to some people sitting on their stoop.

When Debono explains in Maltese that I've come from America to find out what the locals think of the African immigrants, one woman named Rita asks him,
WHAT SHOULD WE SAY?
THAT WE'RE FOR THEM OR AGAINST THEM?

She laughs when she realizes I understand the language, but then she gets right to it...
YESTERDAY ONE OF THEM— ABOUT 12 A.M., WHEN MY 11-YEAR-OLD NEPHEW WAS SITTING ON THE SOFA PLAYING WITH THE COMPUTER— ONE OF THEM OPENED THE DOOR AND WALKED IN,
Her sister chased off the man, Rita says.
Victor has a message for the immigrants.
AT LEAST TURN YOUR BACK WHEN YOU PEE.
J. SACCO 9.09

Manuel drives a bus, and so many blacks use it, he says, that the Maltese won't get on board.
He says one bus driver was beaten by Africans when he told them the bus was already full up.
IT'S LIKE YOU'RE SPEAKING TO AN ANIMAL.
EVEN AN ANIMAL UNDERSTANDS "FULL UP."

Says Carmen:

AT NIGHT THEY PASS BY, THREE OR FIVE OF THEM...

THEY CARRY BOOM-BOXES, OR THEY'RE SPEAKING ON THEIR MOBILES.*

YIYIYIYII!

MOCK AFRICAN LANGUAGE

*MOBILES: CELL PHONES

OBAMA IS GOING TO TAKE THEM ALL!

TELL HIM TO TAKE THEM ALL!

Debono explains that Marsa is a community where "everyone trusts each other," and it has become unnerved by the great number of constantly "changing faces" in the open center. But crime hasn't increased, he says, so he tries to calm the fears of his constituents.

I'M AGAINST THESE [PEOPLE] COMING OVER... BECAUSE I'M SEEING THEY WILL ONE DAY BE INFLUENTIAL IN MALTA AND IT WILL HAPPEN AS ELSEWHERE, IN FRANCE AND BELGIUM, WHERE THEY CAUSE TROUBLE, SMASHING CARS...
LORRY

I DON'T REALLY HAVE ANYTHING AGAINST THEM. I'M CAPABLE OF EMPATHIZING WITH THEM... I UNDERSTAND IT'S AN ISSUE FOR MALTA, BUT I THINK IT'S AN EXAGGERATED THREAT.
MATTHEW

JUST LOOK WHAT THEY DID IN OTHER COUNTRIES ...LOOK AT THE AMERICAN PRISONS. EIGHTY OR 90 PERCENT [OF THE INMATES] ARE NEGROES... IT'S A FACT. [I'M] NOT JUDGING THEM.
CHARLES
J. SACCO 9-09

No man in Malta strikes the anti-immigrant chord as ruthlessly as the self-styled "racialist" visionary Norman Lowell, who is serving a two-year suspended sentence for hate speech.

THE VISIONARY
WE'LL BOOT THEM OUT, OF COURSE.
VERY VERY SIMPLE OPERATION.
WE JUST DUMP THEM INTO QUARRIES... [UNDER] THE BLISTERING SUN THERE, THE PELTING RAIN, AND JUST DROP BREAD AND WATER TO THEM.

WITHIN SIX WEEKS THEY'LL BE CRYING TO BE SENT BACK.

While most Maltese roll their eyes —or gasp— when I bring up Lowell's name, his withering attacks on the African influx resonate with many, even those not willing to swallow his brand of extremism whole.

In fact, Lowell's wider world view, which blames the Jews for most of the world's ills (including the African migrations), holds up Hitler as "The Hero," and envisions a Latin-speaking, all-white empire (Imperium Europa), is generally unknown to the Maltese, few of whom have read his incendiary books.
IMPERIUM EUROPA LOGO
CREDO
JPS
SUBTITLED: "A BOOK FOR THE VERY FEW"
SUBTITLED: "THE BOOK THAT CHANGED THE WORLD."
IMPERIVM EVROPA
Lowell received 4,500 Maltese votes in the 2009 European Parliament elections, triple his tally in a previous contest.
That would be a significant number in a Maltese general election, which are often decided by a few thousand votes.
Though many dismiss Lowell's showing as a protest vote, his and other right-wing voices have induced many mainstream politicians to assert their own anti-immigrant credentials. The African arrivals are now Malta's number one political issue.
At a cafe near St. Anton Gardens, on a scorchingly hot day that saw the landing of 44 more Africans on Malta, Lowell describes the rise of his Imperium Europa movement.
AT FIRST WE ... WERE DENIGRATED, LAUGHED AT, IGNORED, TREATED VERY BADLY BY THE MEDIA. BUT EVENTUALLY WE MANAGED TO RAISE A CONSCIOUSNESS IN THE PEOPLE ...
EVERY BOATLOAD LIKE THE ONE THAT LANDED THIS MORNING IS AN ALARM BELL TO THE PEOPLE.
J. SACCO 9.09

"We've ended with a mess. Nobody knows how many there are here...
"The Nigerians push drugs," he claims. "The Somalis stab everyone in sight."
Lowell has written, "Unless drastic measures are taken to stop the rot now, within 50 years Malta will become the Haiti of the Mediterranean."

HAITI WAS THE PEARL OF THE CARIBBEAN UNDER THE FRENCH. THE BLACKS TOOK OVER AND LOOK AT HAITI NOW.
I MEAN, THE BLACK MAN CAN'T EVEN RUN A NUGGET SHOP, LET ALONE A COUNTRY.
A NUGGET SHOP?
NUGGET IS THE BLACK BOOT POLISH.

"This is a racial war on a planetary scale," Lowell tells me, "and it's a cultural war, a war between civilizations."
In a war, he says, "traitors are shot."
He rails against the Jesuits and other advocates of the immigrants in Malta.
When the "day of reckoning comes," he has written, "there will not be enough lampposts" for the "traitorous bastards."

THAT'S THE ARTISTIC NORMAN LOWELL SPEAKING. IT'S NOT LITERAL, OF COURSE.
J. SACCO 9.09

But someone has taken the extreme right's message to heart.
Arsonists have targetted the homes or property of those considered sympathetic to the immigrants, including journalists, Jesuits, and a lawyer.
Our interview concluded, Lowell and I walk through the gardens, where he spots a black man with three children.
DO YOU SEE?
THEY ARE BREEDING FURIOUSLY IN OUR MIDST.
IT'S THE SUPPLANTING OF OUR POPULATION BY AN INVADING, ALIEN ONE...
BREEDING FURIOUSLY!
THEY CUSS YOU IN THEIR LANGUAGE WHEN YOU PASS. MOST OF THE WOMEN THEY COVER THEIR NOSE.
CLEMENT
MALTESE PEOPLE ARE RACIST... THE MALTESE BELIEVE IF YOU'RE AN AFRICAN IMMIGRANT, YOU ARE NOT SCHOOLED AT ALL. THEY LOOK DOWN ON YOU.
TEMITOPE
I BELIEVE IF THERE WOULD BE MORE IMMIGRANTS THEY WOULD STOP [THEIR ABUSE]. BECAUSE IF WE HAVE MORE NUMBERS, WE WILL TAKE ACTIONS.
YOUSEF
THERE IS NO CONNECTION BETWEEN MALTESE AND AFRICANS. IF YOU MEET THEM, SOME RESPECT YOU. MOST, THEY INSULT YOU.
ABDULLAH
J. SACCO 9.09

THE ERITREAN
He will not give me his name.
He says his family would be at risk if his identity were revealed.
I tell him to make up a name for me, anything, "John," if he likes.
OKAY.
"JOHN."

John would certainly be in danger back in his homeland. In 2002 Malta forcibly returned more than 220 Eritreans; they were immediately imprisoned on their arrival. Many were tortured, and some died from their mistreatment.

John's long, hard journey to Malta began in 2001 when he and thousands of other University of Asmara students refused an Eritrean government order to work the whole summer without pay.

More than 2,000 students, including John, were arrested and loaded onto trucks.
J. SACCO 9.09

WE WERE TAKEN TO WIA AND GELALO, [WHICH ARE] PRISONS IN THE EASTERN PART OF THE COUNTRY... WHERE THE TEMPERATURE IS MORE THAN 45, 44, 43 DEGREES CENTIGRADE* ALWAYS.
*109-113°F
But first they were left in the open, in the summer sun, without food for four days, he says.
"During this time ...two of the students died from heat stroke."
After a few weeks of incarceration, "one by one we were asked to apologize in front of a gun," he says.
"It is not an apology you feel on the inside, but you have to do it to save your life."
The students thought the matter was closed, "but [the government] had long term plans for how to deal with us," he says. They were mobilized for national service.
John spent six months at hard labor.
J. SACCO 9.09

He had been on track for a university job, which normally would have counted as national service. Instead he was next ordered into the army even though he had already fulfilled his military obligation. His transfer requests were turned down.
Three years went by.
"I was assigned to a place where I could do nothing... I had no job... I was in the military because it was a punishment."

Finally, he publically confronted an officer about his situation.
I'M NOT ASKING TO WORK FOR MONEY...
I NEED TO BE ASSIGNED TO A PLACE WHERE I CAN CONTRIBUTE.
"I [knew] that it is risky to speak in a meeting in Eritrea because there is no freedom of expression at all."

He was arrested and jailed the same day.

Upon his release a month later, he was told his annual leave had been rescinded.
John ignored the restriction to attend the wedding of his sister.

The military police were now looking for him. He decided to flee the country.

J. SACCO 10·09

"You have to state on the piece of paper from which division of the army you are [from]... So they can simply call and check, if they want."

For about 800 Euros, a smuggler guided him across the Sudanese border.

"You have to run...

"I left at 7 o'clock in the evening, and it took me the whole night..."

He turned himself in to the Sudanese police, who released him three days later to the desolate U.N. refugee camp in Kassala.

Almost nothing was provided, he says, and Eritrean forces were known to raid the camp to drag refugees back across the border.

J. SACCO 10.09

He decided to leave Kassala for the Sudanese capital, Khartoum, with a one-week pass.
"You [are] not allowed to simply leave and stay in Khartoum. You pay some money and you hand in your [U.N.] ID card to the police, just to make sure you will come back."
But John knew he would not be returning to Kassala for his ID.
Once in Khartoum "if [the police] arrested you for some reason, if you didn't have a residence card, there [was] a risk of deportation...
"Without having legal status you don't feel safe to simply live.
"You feel that everyone is looking at you...
"If you see the police ...you go far [to] the other side."
He stayed with an Eritrean friend, but John couldn't speak Arabic or find a job.
"I could not see any future."
His family sent him money to reach Europe.
THEY KNEW THAT THE SAHARA DESERT AND THE MEDITERRANEAN ARE RISKY. I MIGHT DIE ON THE WAY.
BUT... IF I WAS DEPORTED BACK TO ERITREA, THEY KNEW WHAT WOULD HAPPEN TO ME...
J. SACCO 10·09

He paid Eritrean contacts $200 to pass him along to Sudanese smugglers, who had gathered a group of would-be migrants—Eritreans, Ethiopians, Somalis, and Sudanese.

HOW DID YOU TRAVEL?
THERE WERE THREE CARS. WE WERE...MORE THAN 100 PEOPLE.
100 PEOPLE IN THREE CARS? HOW IS IT POSSIBLE?
IT IS DIFFICULT FOR SOMEONE TO BELIEVE THIS.
He found himself hanging on to the roof of a Land Cruiser.
"You simply have nothing to do.
"You simply push one another.
"You simply go like that."

After traveling three days and nights they were handed over to Libyan smugglers in the middle of the desert.

Each of the migrants had to pay another $300.
J. SACCO 10·09

After 12 days, when they were almost out of food, the Libyans returned with 100 additional migrants.

"We were ready to fight the Libyans," says John.

WE DON'T TRUST YOU ANYMORE.

The Libyans agreed to take the first group onward, and two days later passed them off to another band of smugglers, who charged each person an additional $50.

"It was the Sahara desert. We didn't want to stay even for one [more] hour in the desert. So we gave [the] money."

In a village outside of Benghazi, John was parceled off with about 20 others to a middleman "who bought us, like a commodity" and who would now sell his trafficked guests to another set of smugglers, but not before charging the migrants $200 each himself.

At last they reached Tripoli, but "Tripoli was the most horrible place I saw on my journey. It was very hostile. The police, the people. Very, very, very hostile towards immigrants.

He was staying with 200 other migrants in a building owned by an Ethiopian trafficker.

John decided he would be safer elsewhere. He moved to the outskirts of the city.

He lay low for months and then paid $1,000 to an Eritrean who put him in contact with Libyans who could facilitate a Mediterranean crossing.

J. SACCO 10.09

The Libyans took him into a hiding place which began filling up with Africans hoping to make the same voyage. The 25 days there were tense, he says, with their hosts sometimes threatening to throw them all into the street.

John had a space on the second boat due to leave that morning.

Despite the fate of the first vessel, he and the others pressed the Libyans to let them attempt the crossing.

The "captain," a Ghanain, insisted he knew what he was doing.
"There is no way to check whether he knows or not ...You just pray that he knows."
THERE ARE PEOPLE WHO SIMPLY GO LIKE THIS IN THE MEDITERRANEAN, AND THEY SPEND THREE OR FOUR DAYS AND FINISH.
Estimates for the number of Africans who have perished trying to cross the sea range from the hundreds to more than 10,000.
J. SACCO 10-09
"[The Libyans] gave us wrong information.
"They told us, 'After eight hours you will find Malta... and then ...turn one degree north and you will be there in Sicily.'
"And we traveled eight hours and we saw nothing.
"We continue,
"we continue,
"we continue...
"We traveled the whole day,
"the whole night,
"without stopping,
"without switching off the motor.
"And we traveled the whole day again.

"At about 3 o'clock we saw Malta.
"And [some] thought this must be Sicily [because] we traveled so long.
"But we all agreed that it was not a matter of choice:
"We saw a land mass and we had to land.
"There were people swimming.
"I jumped out of the boat and asked a guy.
"And he told me I am in Malta.
J. SACCO 10.09
"And we stayed on the beach till the police came."

DETENTION
Once they land in Malta, all "irregular immigrants" are locked up and guarded in closed detention centers. Only those considered vulnerable—minors and pregnant women, for example—are fast-tracked out.
John, the Eritrean who arrived in Malta in 2006, remembers,
NOBODY TELLS YOU ABOUT YOUR OBLIGATIONS OR YOUR RIGHTS... NOBODY EXPLAINS WHAT IS GOING TO HAPPEN.
IT IS REALLY STRESSFUL [FOR] DETAINEES AND CREATES A SYSTEM OF FRUSTRATION... YOU LOSE HOPE.
"[We] are people who are in need of help.
"On the contrary, they create a feeling that we are criminals and we need to be guarded by soldiers.
"[The detention centers] should be [staffed by] civilians and those who know how to take care of asylum seekers, who are victims of persecution and rape and all these things..."
ZAMMIT
J. SACCO 11.09

Carmelo Mifsud Bonnici, Minister of Justice and Home Affairs, who is most responsible for policy regarding immigrants, tells me,
THE DETENTION POLICY IS ODIOUS FOR US...BUT IT IS A NECESSITY.
He says the immigrants are an "unknown factor," that for "security reasons" they have to be screened to determine their backgrounds as "the majority do not have identification."
I CANNOT [ALLOW]...PERSONS RUNNING AROUND OUR STREETS WITH NO ACCOMMODATION...
KNOCKING ON DOORS TO GET FOOD,
WITHOUT ANY IDEA WHERE THEY CAME FROM,
AND WITH THE BIG IDEA THAT EUROPE IS AN EL DORADO.
Because deep in the government's heart is the suspicion that many if not most arrivals are economic migrants and not, as almost 100 percent of them claim, victims of war or persecution and that they often falsify their stories to wrangle some form of humanitarian protection—and legal status—from their reluctant hosts.
Refugee Commissioner Mario Friggieri, who runs the busy office that receives and decides on applications for asylum, tells me,
IT IS EASY TO SAY, 'I WAS IN MY COUNTRY AND I WAS PERSECUTED FOR MY POLITICAL OPINION...'
ANYBODY CAN SAY THAT.
YOU HAVE TO PROVE IT.
J. SACCO 11.09

The asylum application process has always been difficult and frustrating, but it was once downright chaotic.
In a group of recently landed immigrants, John was the only one who could properly understand the English-language preliminary questionnaire.
I FILLED [OUT] MINE, AND I FILLED IT OUT FOR ABOUT 30 PEOPLE WHO WERE IN MY ROOM.
J. SACCO 11.09
"There were some people from Sudan, and I couldn't communicate properly with them in Arabic.
"I didn't know myself that [the preliminary questionnaire] is very important and is a base for the asylum application."
About 55 percent of asylum applications are approved for some sort of humanitarian status,
sometimes in the form of the Geneva Convention's strictly defined refugee designation,
but more often through the European Union's more provisional "subsidiary protection" category.
APPROVED
4%
51%
REJECTED
45%
Those whose applications are not successful are subject to deportation, a complicated procedure, not easily followed through, that involves obtaining travel documents from countries of origin.
Friggieri insists that each case is evaluated on its own merits, but immigrants from the conflict-ridden Horn of Africa are far more likely to get protection in Malta than those from countries that are merely "poor [and whose] governments are unstable."

Malta now separates detainees who are most likely to be rejected —West Africans —from those who stand a good chance— East Africans. When the hopefuls and the hopeless intermingled, the former sometimes lauded it over the latter, I'm told, which led to fighting between nationalities.
The Maltese government turns down my request to visit the detention center at Safi, which is "dedicated to rejected asylum seekers."
Lt. Col. Brian Gatt, who heads the Detention Service, the joint force of police and army personnel who guard the detainees, tells me,
THE PROBLEM WITH SAFI IS THAT IF THEY SEE A JOURNALIST, THEY GO BERSERK.
THEY COME OUT WITH POSTERS. THEY MAKE A LOT OF NOISE.
THE TENSION RISES VERY QUICKLY.
In fact, the model facility I'm allowed to visit, Ta' Kandja, had its own riot just three weeks earlier.
"There were 315 Somalis trying to break out," Gatt says. The guards were unarmed, he adds, "so obviously we came to blows."
The Somalis were demanding immediate release.
(Those granted some form of humanitarian protection are generally released within about six months. Those turned down may remain detained for a maximum of a year and a half.)
J. SACCO 11.09

It's calm, however, when I visit the Somali women locked up in Ta'Kandja.

They immediately crowd around me for news of their cases, thinking I am from the Office of the Refugee Commission.

As one of the women fans me — it's rather warm in there — another walks up to show me her badly scarred arm.

Doesn't this prove she fled a war?

Shouldn't this be her ticket to status?

Because not even the Somalis can count on protection. In this room, 20 of 44 women have already had their asylum applications rejected.

I don't tell her that of the thousands of asylum seekers in Malta who have appealed their rejections, "less than ten" have seen their decisions overturned, according to Refugee Commissioner Friggieri.

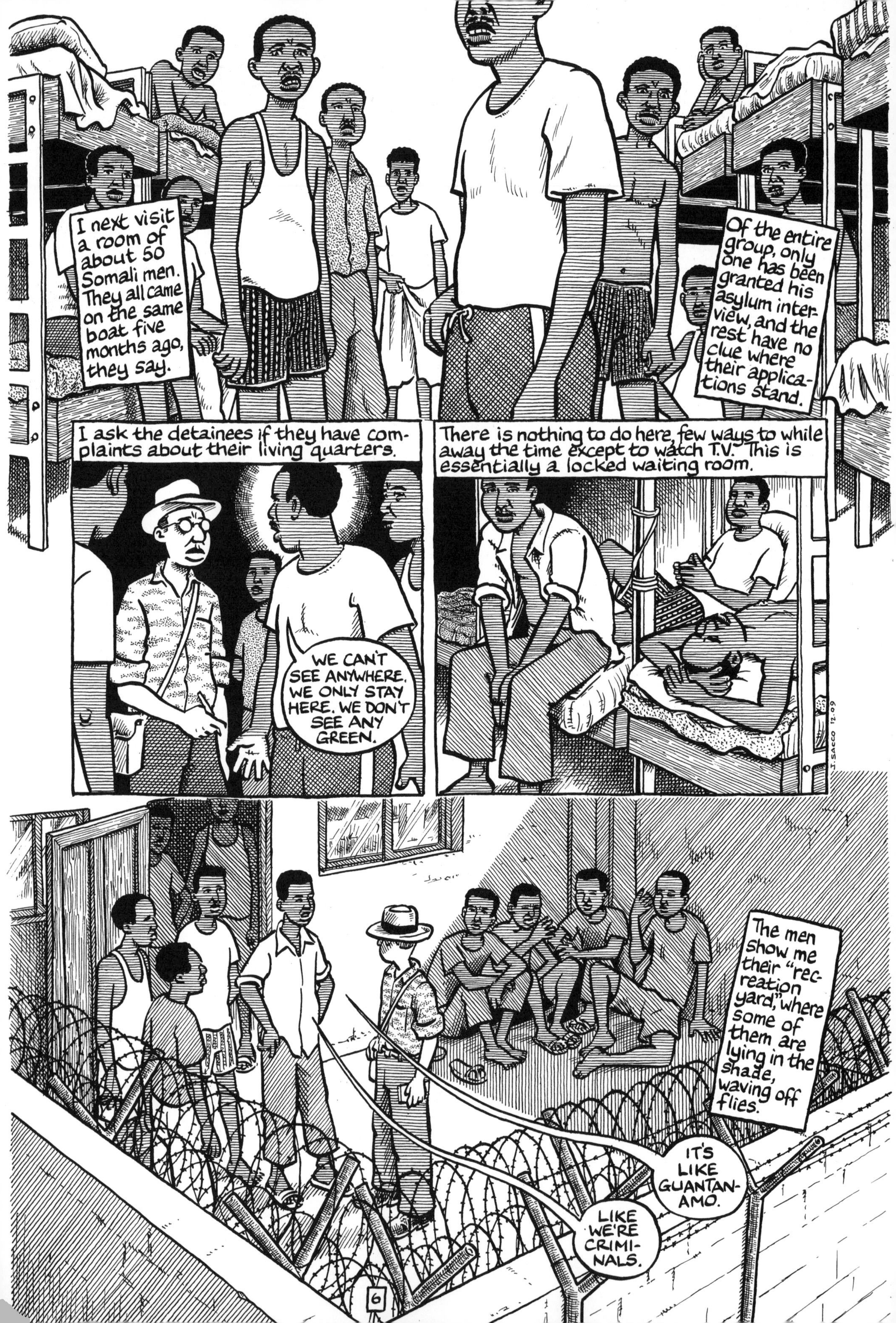
I next visit a room of about 50 Somali men. They all came on the same boat five months ago, they say.
Of the entire group, only one has been granted his asylum interview, and the rest have no clue where their applications stand.
I ask the detainees if they have complaints about their living quarters.
WE CAN'T SEE ANYWHERE. WE ONLY STAY HERE. WE DON'T SEE ANY GREEN.
There is nothing to do here, few ways to while away the time except to watch T.V. This is essentially a locked waiting room.
J. SACCO 12.09
The men show me their "recreation yard," where some of them are lying in the shade, waving off flies.
IT'S LIKE GUANTANAMO.
LIKE WE'RE CRIMINALS.

I won't vouch for Ta'Kandja resembling Guantanamo, but several human rights reports have blasted Malta's detention facilities:
"unacceptable from the point of view of human dignity";
"migrants...are not treated as well as incarcerated criminals";
"unacceptable for a civilized country and untenable in Europe";
"disastrous sanitary facilities";
"clearly inhuman and degrading."
Like all Maltese officials I meet, Lt. Col. Gatt scoffs at most criticism of the nation's detention policy and facilities.
AS A GENERAL RULE, THE PEOPLE IN DETENTION ARE TREATED WITH HUMANITY.
He denies they suffer mental health problems due to their prolonged detention.
As to the charges of degraded facilities, Gatt says, "West Africans take pride in keeping their areas clean [but] East Africans don't give a damn ... The majority are Muslim, they are Arab-oriented, and living in squalor...for them is no problem."
In any case, Gatt tells me, Malta has limited resources, and when the immigrants started landing in numbers, "we didn't have any purpose-built structures to accommodate [them]."
Father Joseph Cassar, director of Jesuit Refugee Service, which does advocacy work on behalf of detainees and offers them legal advice, rejects the policy of prolonged detention.
More than 50 percent of detainees are eventually granted protection, he points out,
WHICH MEANS TRULY THEY ARE ASYLUM SEEKERS.
THEY ARE REFUGEES FOR ALL INTENTS AND PURPOSES...
[YET] PEOPLE BEING CONFINED IN DETENTION ARE GENERALLY PERCEIVED TO BE CRIMINALS.
J. SACCO 12·09

Whether or not they finally are deemed worthy of protection, the immigrants are locked up for months, kept under guard, surrounded by barbed wire, handcuffed when taken to hospital...
If irregular immigrants are treated like prisoners, is it any wonder that the Maltese assume they've done something wrong?
OPEN CENTERS
I wander into Tent No. 33 at the Hal Far Tent Village and introduce myself.
A couple of guys from Togo are sharing a pan of rice,
and a Somali named Abdullah is cooking some potatoes.
These men are so-called "freedoms," those immigrants finally released from detention to open centers, the last supervised stop before Malta tells them to fend for themselves.
Abdullah has lived here for a year, and he is "not satisfied" with his accommodations.
He says he's from a city, Mogadishu, and until he was assigned here, he'd only ever seen tents on television.
BEFORE I RAN FROM THE FIGHTING, BUT NOW I WANT TO RUN FROM THE TENTS...
J. SACCO 12·09

Abdullah shows me around.
The tent village, which is isolated in a remote corner of the island, reminds me of desolate refugee camps I've seen elsewhere.
It has 500 immigrants on its roster and needs to make room for 43 new "freedoms" this week.
"Freedoms" are allowed to move around Malta as they wish, but if they are gone too long from their assigned open center, they are struck off the rolls.
Mario Camilleri, the government coordinator at the tent village, tells me,
AFTER EIGHT WEEKS WE RECLAIM THEIR LIVING SPACE.
ONCE THEY'RE OUT OF THE SYSTEM, THEY STAY OUT.
In other words, they will no longer be eligible for a bunk or the modest allowance they receive.
THE GOVERNMENT GIVES US 130 EUROS A MONTH.
The catch is you need to be here three times a week to sign in for the money.
IF YOU MISS [SIGNING] ONE TIME, YOU CAN LOSE 32 EUROS.
And if you find steady employment, you forfeit eligibility for the handout and can never reclaim it, even if you are laid off later.
J. SACCO 12.09

Since most all the men cannot find work, the monthly 130 Euros are crucial. The immigrants must buy their own food and everything else they need.
Abdullah's parents send him money from Somalia for clothes.
He leads me to a friend named Omar. Omar's time in detention and the tents has made him crazy, Abdullah claims.
I'm told Omar is so mentally damaged that he hasn't been signing for his 130-Euro allowance.
Haven't you alerted the staff, Abdullah?
I DID BUT THEY SAY, 'IT'S NOT OUR PROBLEM.'
He asks if there's anything I can do for Omar, and I agree to mention him at the office here myself.
Hoo boy! Looks like I've kicked a hornet's nest!
I didn't know I carried such weight!
Government employees are running into each other to check up on Omar's case!
J. SACCO 12.09

But when Abdullah produces Omar, Camilleri smells a rat.
EVERY DAY IT'S SOME-THING NEW!
GO LOOK AT THE BULLETIN BOARD!
TAKE HIM TO THE CLIN-IC IN FLO-RIANA!
Medical care is free in Mal-ta, and if Abdullah is so interested in his friend's well being, why doesn't he take his pal to get checked up?
HERE WE ARE NOT YOUR PAR-ENTS!
Camilleri tells me the immi-grants are al-ways trying to game the sys-tem, but per-haps no one has a better insight into that than Ahmed Bugri, a Maltese citizen of Ghanaian origin, who manages the Marsa Open Center.
When resi-dents saw he was paying some of them to clean the facility, they "intentionally" threw garbage on the ground, he says.
THE MORE CLEANERS I EMPLOYED, THE MORE IT BECAME DIRTY... THEY LIT-TERED THE CEN-TER TO CREATE EMPLOY-MENT.
J. SACCO 12.09
And could you blame them?
Bugri esti-mates that only about five percent of his resi-dents land a few hours of work on any given day...
and that only ten of the hun-dreds living in Marsa actu-ally are gain-fully employed.
The rest of them have nothing to do.
"They just walk up and down, roaming aimlessly," he says.

When small shops and kitchens were opened on site to "empower" the residents, a class of operators began treating the businesses as their own property, even selling "ownership" for thousands of Euros.

BEFORE A PERSON RECEIVES HIS CHECK, HE'S ALREADY SPENT IT.

Bugri says he is battling to wrest control of the businesses from their "owners"—many of whom live off site—and is creating a cooperative that will let everyone benefit.

J. SACCO 12.09

There are ethnic tensions at the open center as well.

"All the shops were owned by Somalis," he says. "All the best rooms were Somali... And so they pushed the West Africans and Ethiopians to the back [rooms].

"There are fights, but the Somalis are the majority so they always win the fight."

Whatever its problems, the centrally-located Marsa Open Center, with its restaurants, shops, mosque, chapel, internet cafe, and playing field, is a focal point of African life in Malta and a short walk from the prime gathering spot for day laborers.

African men assigned to other open centers, especially the uncomfortable tent village and a converted airplane hangar in far-off Hal Far, tend to congregate here.

They often spend the night.

In fact,

ALL OF THEM ARE MOVING TO MARSA.

AND THAT'S BECOME OUR NIGHTMARE...

WE'RE SUPPOSED TO HAVE 700 PEOPLE IN MARSA; WE HAVE 1,500...

OUR DATA BASE IS A HOAX. IT DOESN'T TALLY.

J. SACCO 12-09

Malta's policy has essentially created wide cracks for "freedoms" to fall through. Technically, the maximum period the immigrants are allowed to stay at the open centers is one year.

After that their monthly allowance is stopped and they are expected to move out and make it on their own.

Minister Mifsud Bonnici doesn't seem moved by my bleeding-heart concern for their future.

THEY JUST PARK THEMSELVES IN THOSE [CENTERS], AND THEY STAY THERE EXPECTING THE GOVERNMENT TO DO SOMETHING FOR THEM.

THEY HAVE TO FIGHT TO LIVE IN THE WESTERN WORLD...

IF YOU DO NOT PUSH THEM TO DO THIS, THEY DO NOT MOVE.

J. SACCO 12·09

THEY BRING THEIR ANGER BACK TO THE CENTER.
YOU THINK THERE IS PEACE, BUT UNDERNEATH IT'S SIMMERING.
THAT'S WHY THE MALTESE DON'T FEEL SECURE, AND I DON'T BLAME THEM.
"We are waiting on a time bomb..."
CONVERSATION
IT'S A CIRCLE.
IF YOU GIVE THEM GOOD ACCOMMODATION AND YOU TEACH THEM AND GIVE THEM OPPORTUNITIES, THEY'LL CALL THEIR RELATIVES AND TELL THEM TO COME OVER.
WHO [ELSE] ARE THEY CALLING ON THOSE MOBILES?
YOU KNOW IT'S NOT TRUE THAT THE GOVERNMENT GIVES THEM FREE MOBILES.
AND ONLY THOSE WHO ARE IN THE OPEN CENTERS WHO ARE NOT WORKING GET 130 EUROS A MONTH.
130 EUROS? IS THAT FAIR?
MY STIPEND AS A STUDENT IS 60 EUROS A MONTH.
I SHOULD GO AND BE AN ILLEGAL IMMIGRANT.
J. SACCO 12.09

I'M NOT A RACIST, BUT THEY'RE TAKING WORK... THEY'RE WORKING MORE THAN EIGHT HOURS A DAY FOR VERY LITTLE MONEY, FOR POCKET MONEY...
THEY ARE WORKING LIKE SLAVES.
ROSARIO
FIRST OF ALL, THEY CAME HERE TO TAKE OUR WORK... THEY WORK FOR LESS FOR A LONG TIME. THEY WORK WITHOUT SICK LEAVE, WITHOUT CONDITIONS.
BENNY
...SMALL COMPANIES GO AND BRING THREE OR FOUR IMMIGRANTS... AND IF SOMETHING HAPPENS TO THE IMMIGRANTS, NO PROBLEM, THEY BRING ANOTHER ONE.
SALVU
WORK
It's early afternoon, and two Nigerians break off from the men drinking beer and whiskey in one of Marsa's small parks.
Their names are Yousef and Clement, but before I can get anything else out of them, they want to know,
ARE YOU MALTESE?
WE DON'T LIKE MALTESE.
They got out of detention last week, but they carry an atmosphere of utter dejection about them.
They rose before dawn to take the bus from Hal Far to this side of the island and have been looking for a job all day.
IF YOU ENTER AND ASK FOR A JOB, THEY START LAUGHING AT YOU.
WE ARE GOING TO DIE OF HUNGER HERE.
WE ARE CONFUSED.
ALL DAY WE ARE CONTINUOUSLY TREKKING.
They've just walked from Sliema to Marsa in the boiling sun to save on bus fare.
J. SACCO 12.09

Both men have been designated "rejects," meaning their asylum applications have been turned down.
Unlike immigrants granted humanitarian status, they can only get a work permit if a potential employer agrees to jump through bureaucratic hoops to sponsor them.
In other words: fat chance!
Their only hope is off-the-books day labor.
THEY ABANDON US HERE.
But surely the government has given you part of your monthly allowance as a start.
THEY GAVE US 24 EUROS TO BUY OUR CLOTHES, OUR FOOD, EVERYTHING.
WE DON'T HAVE POTS. WE DON'T HAVE GAS. THAT 24 EUROS CANNOT BUY POTS AND PLATES.
WE USE THE MONEY TO EAT IN RESTAURANTS.
Couldn't you take advantage of the free job training or educational benefits Malta claims to provide?
IF I START SCHOOL NOW... WHO WILL PAY TO FEED ME?
OUR TALENTS WILL DIE WITH US HERE.
J. SACCO 12-09

They want to move to mainland Europe, but,
WE HAVE NO PERMISSION TO LEAVE THIS COUNTRY...
Only those with humanitarian protection can acquire temporary travel papers.
There is another way out: enlisting a smuggler to get them to Italy.
Even though Italy has cracked down hard on irregular immigrants—
it even turns back boats in international waters before any passenger can land and ask for asylum
—perhaps one can keep a step ahead of the police and disappear into the African communities there or further north, across the Alps.
Such is this woman's hope.
She says she's fled from Darfur, but the man who introduces us thinks she's actually from Chad.
She is a "double reject," meaning the Refugee Appeals Board let the negative verdict on her asylum application stand.
Her son had himself smuggled from Malta to Italy, and maybe she can follow in the same way.
Meanwhile, she is struggling to pay for the apartment she shares.
She just worked 11 days as a chambermaid and received only 130 Euros.
Yes, the hotel manager ripped her off, but without a work permit she has no recourse.
Our mutual acquaintance worries she will drift into prostitution.
J. SACCO 12.09

A few days later, I get up early to join immigrants, mostly West African "rejects," waiting near the Marsa Open Center for a day labor job.
These two guys, Charles and Samuel, are from Nigeria, and, like the woman I'd met recently, they have no work permit. They tell me how Maltese employers take advantage of the fact.
THEY WILL USE YOU TO WORK, AND THEN THEY ASK YOU FOR A WORK PERMIT AND WON'T PAY YOU [WITHOUT IT].
IF WE CALL THE POLICE, THEY WILL ASK FOR THE WORK PERMIT [TOO].
They don't have a legal leg to stand on, and the competition, as the occasional car stops to scoop up a worker or two, is fierce.
TWENTY OR 30 PEOPLE RUN TO THE CAR.
AND THEN THEY WILL [OFFER] WHAT THEY LIKE.
BECAUSE THERE ARE MANY OF US, IF YOU DON'T AGREE [TO THE WAGE], SOMEONE ELSE WILL.
J. SACCO 12-09
SOME STOP AND WHEN YOU RUN TO THE CAR THEY SAY, 'FUCK YOU!'... AND JUST GO.
Neither of these men have had much luck finding work.
Samuel says he has worked only three times in the month since he was released from detention.
IS THERE ANY PLACE YOU CAN DIRECT US TO GET A JOB?

I visit another group of men further up.
Mohammed from Ghana is one of the lucky ones.
He says he's been employed two weeks running as a plasterer, earning 20-25 Euros a day.
He is waiting for his employer to pick him up.
SOME PEOPLE STAY HERE FOR MONTHS, WEEKS, AND THEY HAVEN'T WORKED ONCE.
As if to prove his point, a young man from Togo steps forward.
He hasn't worked at all since he was made a "freedom" one month ago.
He comes here every day to try his luck, meaning he hasn't been signing in for his allowance at Hal Far.
Expressing the frustration of the West Africans in Malta who are "rejects,"
who are subject to deportation,
who can neither obtain a work permit nor papers to reach another European country,
who will disappear into Malta's mini-ghettoes with no legal status or prospects at all,
Mohammed says,
WE HAVE ALL PASSED THROUGH THE SEA. WE ARE ALL HUMAN BEINGS.
THEY DON'T HAVE TO TREAT SOMALIS BETTER THAN US.
WE ARE ALL CREATED BY GOD.
HOW DO YOU EXPECT ME TO EAT?
DO YOU WANT ME TO ROB?
YOU CAN'T TELL ME, 'YOU DON'T HAVE A PERMIT, YOU CAN'T WORK.'
WE ARE SUFFERING EVEN MORE THAN IN OUR OWN COUNTRY.
J. SACCO 12.09

But suddenly a van stops, and the guy from Togo doesn't wait to hear out Mohammed's lament.
Only one other fellow seems to have seen the vehicle.
There's a quick discussion with the driver, and then both men hop in.
Our Togolese pal has landed his first job.
YOU CAN'T INTEGRATE THEM... WE'RE TOO DIFFERENT.
IN ENGLAND THEY DON'T WANT THEM TO PUT A CROSS IN THE SCHOOL*...IF THEY DON'T WANT TO SEE THE CROSS, THEY SHOULD STAY IN SOMALIA
THIS COUNTRY IS OURS, NOT THEIRS.
ROMINA
*ADDITIONALLY, IN NOV. 2009, A EUROPEAN COURT TOLD ITALY TO REMOVE CRUCIFIXES FROM THE WALLS OF STATE SCHOOLS.
I DON'T SEE ANY PROSPECT OF SETTLING DOWN [IN MALTA].
I WANT TO GO TO A COUNTRY WHERE I FEEL I BELONG...OR BACK TO ERITREA, IF PEACE COMES TO MY COUNTRY.
IT'S TRUE I'M LIVING IN MALTA, BUT IN REALITY I'M LIVING IN THE AFRICAN COMMUNITY IN MALTA.
JOHN
INTEGRATION
Ahmed Bugri, the manager of the Marsa Open Center, married in Malta and has lived here for almost two decades.
FOR THREE YEARS MY FATHER-IN-LAW TOLD ME HE DIDN'T WANT A BLACK MAN IN HIS FAMILY.
BUT NOW HE'S SEEN ME TAKE CARE OF MY WIFE... AND TAKE CARE OF MY CHILDREN.
NOW HE LOVES ME AS A SON.

But Bugri is not hopeful about the integration of other Africans.
"The Maltese are scared having black people populate this place," he says. "[They] want the migrants out."
J. SACCO 1:10
And the Africans want exactly the same thing:
to get off this small island, to reach the European mainland.
What is the point, asks Minister Mifsud Bonnici, of trying to integrate people who don't want to live here?
...WE DO A LOT OF WORK, WE INVEST A LOT OF TIME, OF MONEY AND RESOURCES ON PERSONS...WHO WE MUST ACCEPT...DO NOT LOOK AT [MALTA] AS THEIR FINAL DESTINATION...
Malta is just their "stepping stone," he insists.
His job is to get the rest of Europe to acknowledge that and take Africans with humanitarian status off Malta's hands.
Mifsud Bonnici warms to the idea of a better life for Africans on the continent.
ONCE YOU ARE IN PORTUGAL, YOU HAVE ACCESS TO SWEDEN OR FINLAND.
YOU CAN GO IN A CAR, AND YOU CAN DRIVE YOUR WAY UP.

One gets the impression the minister would drive them there himself, if only someone would take them, if only the Africans would —in a phrase he repeats over and over—
MOVE ON.
But Mifsud Bonnici is a big-picture man.
He knows the Maltese voters, he knows the budgetary constraints, he needs to ease the pressure on a tiny nation straining under sudden social, cultural, and racial problems generated by wars, poverty, and climate change somewhere far, far away.
Francis Debono, the mayor of Marsa, knows the voters, too.
He and they live cheek-by-jowl with hundreds of African men at the open center.
He is much less hopeful than the minister that mainland Europe will integrate great numbers of Malta's Africans.
SOME OF THEM ARE GOING TO BE HERE FOR YEARS...
IN THE END, THE FEAR [OF] AND PITY FOR THEM ENDS.
BECAUSE YOU GET USED TO THEM, AND YOU HAVE TO LIVE IN THE REALITY THAT EXISTS.
WE ARE NOT TRYING TO INTEGRATE OURSELVES; WE ARE NOT TRYING TO LOOK AT THE FUTURE PROBLEMS.
YOU HAVE TO GIVE THEM SCHOOLS, MOSQUES, HEALTH TREATMENT... EVERYTHING THEY NEED, ACTUALLY.
J. SACCO 1·10

He worries about large concentrations of Africans dominating neighborhoods.
He worries that eventually the chronically underemployed "double rejects" will create criminal organizations.
In fact, he has almost every worry that every Maltese person has about their uninvited guests.
But Debono worries more that Malta is losing its way.
IF YOU HAVE A CHANCE TO HELP PEOPLE GET ON THEIR FEET, THEN YOU MUST.
YOU'RE TALKING ABOUT PEOPLE, NOT GRASS.
J. SACCO 1-10
The Maltese, who play host to hundreds of thousands of European tourists every year, have long taken pride in their reputation for hospitality.
According to the 'Acts' of the apostles, St. Paul was shipwrecked here and struggled through the raging surf onto the island where the natives showed him and the other survivors "unusual kindness."
I reminded one of my relatives of this story and compared the reception of the Africans to that of St. Paul.
She would have none of it.
"But St. Paul was here for a while and left," she said.

Migration, Notes

I thought there was no better place to report on the issue of African migration to Europe than my own birthplace, Malta. For one thing, as a Maltese I figured local people would be less reticent with me about their feelings toward the Africans who had landed on the island. For another, though English is widely spoken there, it is not spoken by everyone, and my fair knowledge of the Maltese language would allow me to operate without a translator. Also, Malta is a small country, one of those places where one can make an appointment with the ministers and officials who are the chief architects and administrators of policy. Finally, this story could be easily told from the perspective of the Africans, who were approachable in the camps and centers where they lived and in the streets while they looked for work. Fortunately, with forty-eight pages, the *Virginia Quarterly Review* gave me plenty of room to cover all these bases. Though obviously my sympathies are with the migrants, who had endured tremendous hardships to reach such an unwelcoming place whatever their reasons for setting out across the Mediterranean Sea, I thought it was incumbent on me to treat the fears and apprehensions of the Maltese people seriously. Few peoples, I'm afraid, are up to the challenge of absorbing large and sudden influxes of outsiders, especially those of a different color. My own people are no better than anyone else.

"The Unwanted" appeared in the *Virginia Quarterly Review* in two parts in the Winter 2010 and Spring 2010 issues.

INDIA

KUSHINAGAR
This is how our story ends:
by Joe Sacco © 2010
Together with my guide, the Indian reporter Piyush Srivastava, I am sitting in a hut blackened by cooking smoke with two men we have gotten to know these last three days.
They are Dalits, once called "Untouchables," the people who perch on the bottommost rung of India's caste system.
In fact, these two,
Bhelu and Sib Charan,
are Musahars, a lowly subcaste even among the Dalits,
and they are hanging onto the planet by their fingernails.
J. SACCO 4.10
Somewhere outside, Brijesh, a local journalist we have brought along to run interference, is doing his best to keep Green Shirt away from us.
Green Shirt has been hounding us since our first visit to the village of Kurwa Dilipnagar, and we strongly suspect he is the village chief's henchman.
IS THAT MAN GOING TO SHOW THE POVERTY OF INDIA AND DEFAME MY VILLAGE?
Today he picked us up the moment we turned the corner to reach the Musahar hamlet of Gurumiha Mafitola.

Green Shirt was born into the Other Backward Classes, an officially designated group of castes who are generally disadvantaged but who consider themselves the human superiors of the Dalits.
Further up the scale are the Forward Castes —Brahmins, Rajputs, and others—before whom Dalits and Backward Classes obligingly bow and scrape.
In rural India especially, the caste-based tiers form daunting barriers to any sort of social or economic mobility and are the ready-made framework around which the vines of inequality twirl and thrive.
As if by right then, Green Shirt can hinder our meeting with the Musahars, he can barge in and try to stop it,
J. SACCO 4.10
and if Brijesh manages to deflect him,
he can't contain a group of higher caste teenagers who suddenly surround the hut and peer over the Dalit women listening in.

We emerge, and as the boys close around us,
our host, Sib Charan, steps forward to address me.
LOOK, IT IS VERY GOOD THAT YOU ARE COMING HERE, BUT SINCE WE ARE NOT GOING ANYWHERE BECAUSE OF YOU—
he means to find work or food
—IT'S A PROB-LEM.
TOMOR-ROW WE WILL NOT MEET.
I'm taken aback. I hadn't considered how our daily visits might be interfering with the grim business of survival here in the Kushi-nagar district of Uttar Pradesh, one of India's poorest states.
But now he ges-tures as if indi-cating the boys among us.
YOU KNOW THE PROB-LEM.
BIG PEOPLE WILL GET ANNOYED.
"Big people." That's a euphemism for those who call the shots in the village, those who perhaps aren't so much wor-ried that we'll glimpse the shameful pov-erty here as get an inkling into what a wonderful busi-ness it can be.
J. SACCO 4.10

The boys escort us back to our car.
They are victorious.
They have chased the prying outsiders from their village.
DALIT PRIDE
Underneath the India of billionaires and Bollywood stars, the India whose growth rate rivals China's, is a country in which more than three-quarters of the population—836 million people—live on less than half a dollar a day and where the prevalence of underweight children is nearly double that of Sub-Saharan Africa.
DELHI
UTTAR PRADESH
KOLKATA
MUMBAI
INDIA
KUSHINAGAR DISTRICT
UTTAR
LUCKNOW
PRADESH
GORAKHPUR
The rural depths of Kushinagar represent the India that neither shines nor sparkles nor even flickers, where most people have next to nothing or nothing and where it is possible, through indebtedness, to have even less.

For the Musahars of the Gurumiha Mafitola hamlet, the Below the Poverty Line definition, which government committees endlessly recalibrate, is a moot point because the issue is not merely poverty, which might be bearable, but hunger.
That is their only concern: food.
The people here don't know how old they are, and few can tell you how their children died—
all the women we ask seem to have lost two or three.
THEY WERE FIVE OR SIX YEARS OLD WHEN THEY DIED. THEY WERE ILL.
THERE WAS NO MEDICINE.
LALI DEVI
There is no religion here and no politics.
ONCE IT'S DECIDED BY THE VILLAGE CHIEF THE ENTIRE VILLAGE AGREES TO IT, AND THAT'S HOW WE VOTE.
WE DON'T KNOW WHAT PARTY IT IS.
They cannot tell us the names of India's prime minister or Uttar Pradesh's chief minister, who is known simply as Mayawati.
Mayawati is a Dalit herself and the self-styled champion of her downtrodden kind.
J. SACCO 4-10

In the state capital, Lucknow, on a scale and at an expense that would make a Pharaoh blush, she has cleared enormous tracts of land on which she has built monuments to Dalit worthies and erected oversized statues of herself.
THE BHIMRAO AMBEDKAR MEMORIAL (WHICH INCLUDES 60 MARBLE ELEPHANTS)
In her fiery speeches she trumpets "Dalit Pride," but here in Kushinagar, the Dalits who bring out chairs for us at our first meeting will not dare to sit with upper caste visitors or a white man.
I mistake the building behind us for one of their homes, but they tell me it's a government school built five years ago.
But the teacher stopped teaching, they say, and he only showed up to shoot the breeze with the men —presumably while still drawing his paycheck.
He stopped coming around all together three months ago, they tell us.
Here they don't see any point in informing the authorities, and they won't send their kids to other schools nearby.
CHILDREN OF THE [HIGHER] CASTES START BEATING THEM...
IT WAS HERE THAT THEY WERE SAFE.
IF THEY OPEN IT AGAIN, [THE CHILDREN] WILL GO.
But Sib Charan's own son tells me he's never been to school before, apparently not even when classes were held here.

Indeed, what good would a little education do? Would it lead anywhere?
What does Sib Charan expect from his kids?
WE ASK THEM TO DO SOMETHING [TO] BRING SOME FOOD.
What does his wife, Suvanti, hope for their children?
I DON'T THINK ANYTHING ABOUT IT.
What does their son, Rajinder, want out of life?
I HAVE NO PLAN.
Here there is no electricity, no toilet, no 21st or 20th or 19th century convenience of any kind.
What the hamlet does have are three hand-operated water pumps, put in about ten years ago, and brick houses.
The houses were paid for by the government under a program named for former prime minister Indira Gandhi.
Sib Charan says the government gave him 25,000 rupees to build, of which 5,000 was scooped off by an official.
Sib Charan and a son pooled their handouts and built this modest structure.
We ask to be invited in.
J. SACCO 4.10

The house is devoid of furnishings.
I am given a brick to sit on.
Mice are running all around us.
Suvanti tells us their bedding is cow fodder spread on the bare concrete floor. They have a few blankets.
Yes, it is very cold in the winter, and she has only two saris.
A sari costs the equivalent of a bit more than $2, but,
WE DON'T HAVE ANY BALANCE AFTER SPENDING ON FOOD.
Food! The topic to end all topics!
I notice four bags of grain.
One of their sons works in a city and brought them some supplies, they say.
Otherwise, they subsist on government-subsidized rations (more about those later), which they pay for with what they earn as agricultural day laborers.
What do they earn when they work?
Fifty or 60 rupees a day, says Sib Charan.
AND IF THEY'RE FEELING ESPECIALLY GENEROUS, THEY PAY 100 RUPEES.*
*100 RUPEES: ABOUT $2.20
J. SACCO 4.10

Here in Kushinagar women can be hired for much less than men, usually 30 rupees per day.
Suvanti says she works for 20. Does she know that the minimum wage is 100 rupees?
WHAT IS THE POINT OF KNOWING IT?
MEN MAKE 100 RUPEES, WOMEN MAKE 20 RUPEES.
HOW DOES IT MAKE A DIFFERENCE IF I KNOW?
In any case, agricultural jobs are steady only during the planting and harvesting season, which she says adds up to just two months a year.
It is March, and the last time there was any such work for most all the Dalits we talk to was in October or November when they brought in the rice crop.
Meanwhile, mechanization is slowly but surely making their labor superfluous.
BEFORE, WE USED TO GET SOME WORK. WE DON'T GET IT NOW...
MOST OF THE WORK IS DONE BY TRACTORS AND MACHINES.
ANGANI DEVI
J. SACCO 5.10
To supplement their pitiful income, a government scheme supposedly provides jobs to the rural poor.
But none of the Dalits we meet worked more than a fraction of the 100 days guaranteed every year, and many had never even heard of the program.

With such meager prospects for earnings, we are still trying to understand how they survive.
THINGS HAVE REACHED A STAGE WHERE WE DON'T EVEN FEEL HUNGER.
But people do feel hunger.
How do they fill their bellies?
FROM HITHER AND THITHER.
Bhelu says they augment their diet with snails and with mud-fish caught by hand from pools of water.
J. SACCO 5.10
Suvanti answers our queries without hesitation:
THE WOMEN GO TO THE FIELDS WHERE THE RATS ARE, AND WE COLLECT THE GRAINS THAT [THEY STORE] IN THEIR HOLES, AND WE BRING THEM HERE.
WE GO THERE EVERY DAY.
Who goes?
Just the women?
ALL OF US!
AND CHILDREN!
EVEN MEN!

There's a commotion outside.

WHAT DID YOU TELL THEM?

And in bursts Green Shirt without a knock or hello.

This is the first time we encounter him.

He steps over the women in the hallway...

and plants himself in front of us.

Our meeting is adjourned!

J. SACCO 5-10

SO MANY SCHEMES

In fact, we find a general skepticism about education.

In some cases a child's labor value trumps whatever are the perceived benefits of sitting in class.

Some of the Musahars we meet in the village of Mainpur are lucky enough to find employment at a local brick kiln.

Mahant Prasad says,

OUR ENTIRE FAMILY GOES THERE ...EXCEPT MY MOTHER...

MY YOUNGEST DAUGHTER IS SEVEN YEARS OLD. SHE GOES ALSO.

At the kilns work is paid by the piece so if the tiniest hands can carry just a single brick at a time, they still would contribute something.

In the same village, we find that some of the Musahars inherited small fields doled out during previous government land redistribution schemes.

But most of them sold their land to buy the necessities their wages cannot cover and to pay off the loans they inevitably must take from money-lending sharks—who charge interest as high as 10 percent per month.

J. SACCO 5.10

Rajdeo sold part of his land to pay off a 10,000-rupee debt.
Can't he eke out some food from the remaining eighth of an acre?
THERE'S NO MONEY ...FOR SEEDS AND FERTILIZER AND ALL THAT.

In Sohrauvana village a mixed group of Dalits from the Chumar sub-caste and their equally poor Muslim neighbors gather in a cow shed to field our questions.
We have been talking for some time when I notice a young woman working her way forward.

Suddenly she is in front of us, demanding to know what all of the commotion is about.
If we are giving out benefits, she wants her name on the list.
I tell her we have come to find out about life here, that we have no benefits to give.
Her name is Astabul Nisha, and she says her husband is "extremely ill."
[THE AUTHORITIES] DON'T GIVE ANYTHING TO US.
WE EAT WHEN WE GET SOME WORK.
WE ARE DEPRIVED OF PRACTICALLY EVERYTHING.
NEITHER GOD NOR MEN, NO ONE IS THERE TO LISTEN TO US.
J. SACCO 5.10

Maybe Ajay Kumar Pandey should listen to her.
Here in Padrauna, Kushinagar's district headquarters, Pandey is the block development officer who, until recently, was responsible for all government aid projects in the area where Astabul Nisha lives.
But unlike her, when he wants something he rings a bell.
PING
A peon trots in,
Pandey gives his orders,
the peon trots out.
Would his guests like coffee or tea?
PING
When his bell begins to sputter,
he winds it up,
making it ready for more ringing.
J. SACCO 6-10
With enormous gusto, Pandey outlines the sweep of government entitlements available to the poor, including a toilet scheme, a brick-housing scheme, a food distribution scheme, a jobs scheme, a self-employment scheme...
ANY PERSON WHO WANTS TO ESTABLISH HIS OWN BUSINESS, WE HELP HIM. THERE IS NO SCARCITY OF FUNDS...
IF THEY NEED TO HAVE WORK, THEY GO TO THE VILLAGE CHIEF, THE SECRETARY OF THE GRAM PANCHAYATS OR DIRECTLY TO ME.
TION TO OPEN A BANK ACCOUNT.
THEY WILL GET A JOB WITHIN 14 DAYS...
Name any problem and he has a campaign, a loan, a subsidy, or an acronym that will make it go away.
In short he proves to us beyond any doubt that Astabul Nisha and people like her are all but frolicking in a forest of solutions.
THERE ARE SO MANY SCHEMES FOR THEM.

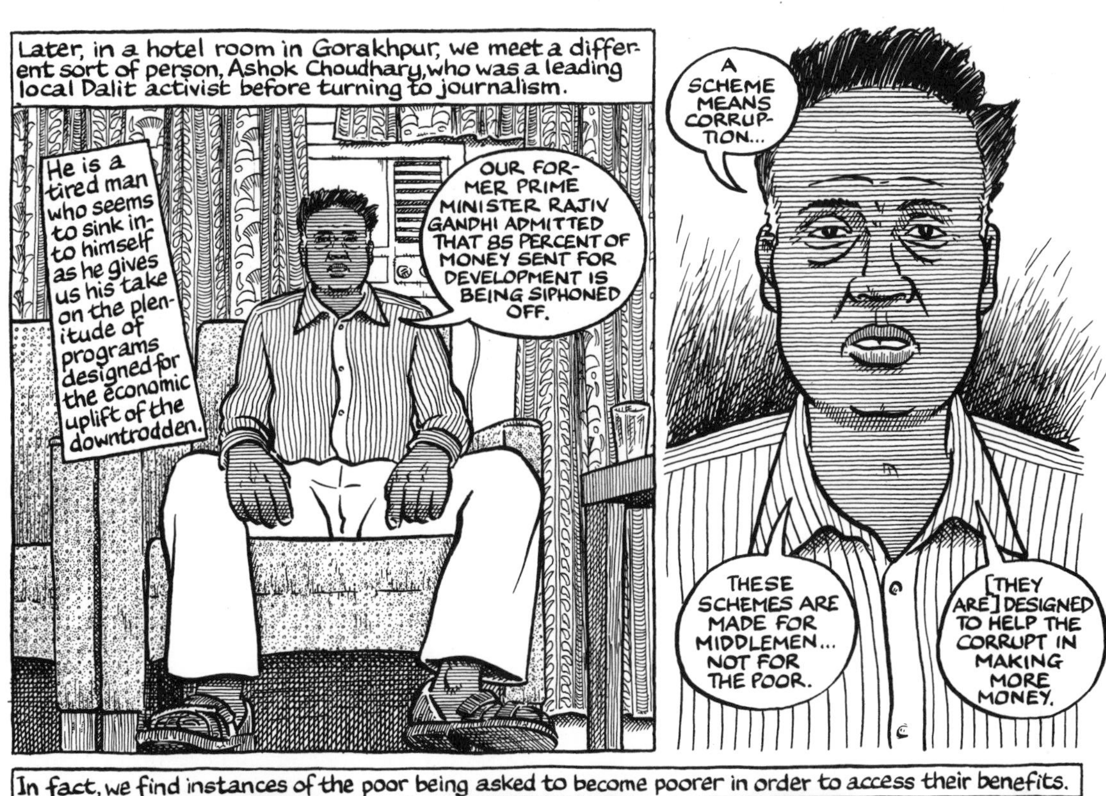
Later, in a hotel room in Gorakhpur, we meet a different sort of person, Ashok Choudhary, who was a leading local Dalit activist before turning to journalism.
He is a tired man who seems to sink into himself as he gives us his take on the plenitude of programs designed for the economic uplift of the downtrodden.
OUR FORMER PRIME MINISTER RAJIV GANDHI ADMITTED THAT 85 PERCENT OF MONEY SENT FOR DEVELOPMENT IS BEING SIPHONED OFF.
A SCHEME MEANS CORRUPTION...
THESE SCHEMES ARE MADE FOR MIDDLEMEN... NOT FOR THE POOR.
[THEY ARE] DESIGNED TO HELP THE CORRUPT IN MAKING MORE MONEY.

In fact, we find instances of the poor being asked to become poorer in order to access their benefits.
Bagmani from Kusumaha village says she has been told by her village chief to hand over 5,000 rupees if she wants to get on the list for a brick house.
SO FAR WE HAVEN'T GIVEN THE BRIBE.

Fatma from Sohrauvana village says she has been eligible for an old-age pension for two years but hasn't drawn a single payment because she hasn't paid a 5,000-rupee bribe.
HER UNSTAMPED PENSION BOOK
Her son was arrested for complaining about this at a village committee meeting.
I WAS A LITTLE LOUD AT THE TIME, AND THAT THEY DIDN'T LIKE.
J. SACCO 6.10

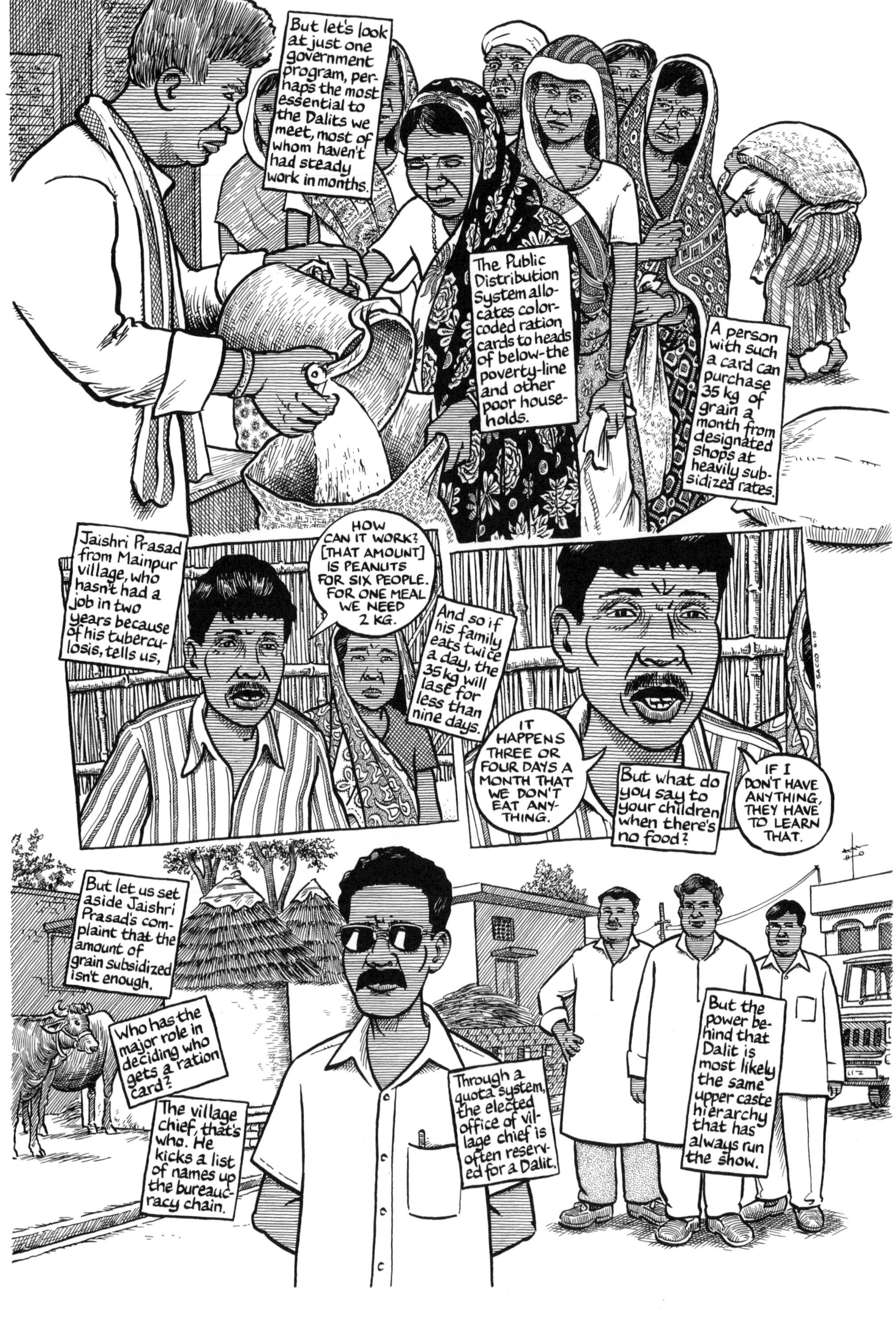
But let's look at just one government program, perhaps the most essential to the Dalits we meet, most of whom haven't had steady work in months.
The Public Distribution System allocates color-coded ration cards to heads of below-the poverty-line and other poor households.
A person with such a card can purchase 35 kg of grain a month from designated shops at heavily subsidized rates.
Jaishri Prasad from Mainpur village, who hasn't had a job in two years because of his tuberculosis, tells us,
HOW CAN IT WORK? [THAT AMOUNT] IS PEANUTS FOR SIX PEOPLE. FOR ONE MEAL WE NEED 2 KG.
And so if his family eats twice a day, the 35 kg will last for less than nine days.
IT HAPPENS THREE OR FOUR DAYS A MONTH THAT WE DON'T EAT ANYTHING.
But what do you say to your children when there's no food?
IF I DON'T HAVE ANYTHING, THEY HAVE TO LEARN THAT.
But let us set aside Jaishri Prasad's complaint that the amount of grain subsidized isn't enough.
Who has the major role in deciding who gets a ration card?
The village chief, that's who. He kicks a list of names up the bureaucracy chain.
Through a quota system, the elected office of village chief is often reserved for a Dalit.
But the power behind that Dalit is most likely the same upper caste hierarchy that has always run the show.

[JUST BECAUSE] SOMEONE... IS A DALIT AND A VILLAGE CHIEF DOESN'T MEAN HE HAS ANY DALIT CONCERNS.
IN SOCIAL AND POLITICAL TERMS, THEY HAVE ALMOST BECOME THE FACILITATORS OF THE TRADITIONAL RICH.
And they can use their position to enrich themselves.
I ask one local journalist, Rakesh Chandra Pandey, who estimates he knows 35 village chiefs personally, if he has met any honest ones.
NO!
THEY ARE 100 PERCENT CORRUPT!
While we can't verify that assertion, we do find numerous instances of village chiefs misusing ration cards.
For example, Ramesh from Kusumaha village says his card is being held by the village chief, who diverts the subsidized rations as he pleases.
SOMETIMES WE DON'T GET [FOOD] REGULARLY.
ON OCCASION THEY GIVE THE FOOD TO SOMEONE ELSE USING OUR CARD.
I WENT TO THE VILLAGE CHIEF, AND HE SAID THE PROBLEM WILL BE SOLVED IN TWO MONTHS.
That was two years ago.
...WE ASKED HIM FOR [THE CARD] AND HE SAYS IT WILL [BE RETURNED], BUT I DON'T KNOW WHEN.
J. SACCO 6-10

In Sohrauvana village, where an adult died of hunger some months ago—
local journalists have documented 45 adult hunger deaths in Kushinagar since 2005
—Ram Pirit pulls up his clothes to show us his withered limbs.
He says the rations here are controlled by the village chief's brother-in-law.
HE GIVES MY SHARE TO OTHER PEOPLE.
SOMETIMES I DON'T HAVE ANYTHING TO EAT.
Ram Pirit's family is kept going by money sent by a relative working as a manual laborer in Mumbai.
Virendra Sharma, standing nearby, claims he's taken on the man behind the village chief.
WE ARE SUPPOSED TO GET 35KG OF FOOD GRAIN, BUT WE ONLY GET 15.
I'M NOT TALKING ABOUT MYSELF...
I TOOK 35 KG...
I CAN FIGHT FOR MY RIGHTS.
THE OTHERS ARE NOT READY TO FIGHT.
WHY DON'T YOU TELL THEM FRANKLY THAT YOU BRIBED HIM.
Bigani, a widow from Mainpur village, tells us,
THE VILLAGE CHIEF SAYS MY [RATION] CARD HAS BEEN CANCELLED.
HE SAYS THERE IS AN ERROR ON MY CARD, AND I SHOULD GO TO THE DISTRICT MAGISTRATE'S OFFICE IN PADRAUNA TO GET IT CORRECTED.
Like most Dalits we meet, Bigani believes that appealing to government officials is a waste of time. All are perceived as corrupt.
I'LL NOT GO ANYWHERE.
She has been forced to buy grain on credit and has sold her land to pay that debt.
J. SACCO 6.10

Everyone we speak to in her village says that only 30 kg of grain is dispensed at the subsidized rate.
Shouldn't it be 35 kg?
WE DON'T QUESTION SUCH THINGS.
WE GET 30 KG OF RICE, AND THAT'S ALL WE KNOW.
And the missing grain?
That can be sold on the open market for a tidy profit.
We hear a motorcycle pull up outside the enclosed area where we're talking.
The village chief has arrived, and he must have overheard some of our conversation.
WHY ARE YOU SAYING ALL THESE THINGS?
DON'T YOU GET YOUR FOOD GRAIN?
Then he roars away, afraid, it seems, to speak to us.
We would also like to meet the village chief of Kurwa Dilipnagar, where we've done most of our fieldwork.
But he breaks our appointments two or three times.
"I'm not running away from you," he assures my guide, Piyush, on the phone, but he soon stops answering our calls all together.
J. SACCO 6·10

I ask Sib Charan and Bhelu whether they see much of him in the hamlet.
HE DOESN'T COME HERE.
Unless it's election time, they say.
Then he "comes to every house" promising better dwellings and land.
THE SONS OF VISHNU
Less than a minute's drive away, the rajas of Kurwa Dilipnagar sit in shady repose and survey their Dalit hirelings beating the seed out of mustard plants.
Of course, they are not really rajas anymore—
India did away with its multitude of princely states at independence
—but one might be forgiven for thinking otherwise upon meeting the Singh brothers, with their palace as a backdrop and their attendants at the ready.
In fact:
WE ARE THE DESCENDANTS OF LORD VISHNU.

This is Upendra, the eldest of six brothers who have reclaimed the run-down, 150-year-old royal residence after the family lived elsewhere for decades. They intend to restore the building to its former luster.
AND IT WILL HAPPEN...
THIS IS OUR IDENTITY. THIS IS OUR ROOT.
The family ruled for 1,000 years, he tells us.
It was a minor dynasty, but in its most glorious period, under the rule of Dilip Narayan Singh, who built the palace and for whom the area was renamed, its territory extended into the neighboring state of Bihar.
Would you rule again, I ask, if you had the chance?
YOU ARE TALKING THE IMPOSSIBLE.
Still, Upendra is happy to rhapsodize about his family's beneficent rule in that officially vanished feudal era.
THE OLDER PEOPLE WHO REMEMBER BEFORE INDEPENDENCE BELIEVE THAT PERIOD WAS BETTER.
THERE WAS DISCIPLINE, THERE WAS HONESTY, THERE WAS CHARACTER.
J. SACCO 6-10

"Earlier, every problem, including that of murder, used to be solved at this door," he says. "We used to [mete out] justice amicably. Now even a minor issue reaches the police."
But Upendra must still be held in some regal regard because Dalit and Other Backward Class villagers come seeking his mediation in family disputes and they respect his verdict, he says.
Have there been any improvements since the passing of the princely states?
Well, yes.
THOSE PEOPLE YOU ARE STUDYING, THE MUSAHARS, THEY HAVE CLOTHES TODAY, BUT JUST TEN YEARS AGO THEY WORE LOINCLOTHS... THEY HAD MUD HOUSES.
NOW EVEN THEIR CHILDREN ARE GOING TO SCHOOL.
I do not interrupt Upendra with the news that the Musahar children living nearby are searching for rat food instead of attending class.
J. SACCO 6.10
In any case, it is time to join his brother, Surendra, accompanied by two attendants, to the spot where a family ancestor reputedly welcomed the Buddha, who, sick with poison, was on his way to the village of Kushinagar to die.

On the way Surendra tells us,
WHAT-EVER YOU SEE IS OURS.
He is talking about land.
Land!
From which the grain grows!
And the family controls a vast expanse though, technically, it no longer retains title to more than a fraction.
In one of its wavering efforts to address inequality, the government redistributed land belonging to former royal households, and it took 1,500 acres from the Singhs to lease to those with no property.
According to Upendra,
AN INJUSTICE WAS DONE TO US.
Hundreds of the landless, including many from the Musahar hamlet, were the beneficiaries.
The holdings were too small to provide a living, but they were something.
We were shown their government-issued proofs of tenancy.
But fat good these documents did. The rajas and others who had property taken from them defied the land transfers violently.
J. SACCO 6.10

Said Banka,
SOME OF [US] WHO TRIED TO TAKE POSSESSION OF OUR LAND WERE BEATEN AND THROWN OFF.
THEY EVEN BEAT THOSE WHO ARE STRONG AMONG US.
IT IS OBVIOUS WE FEAR THEM.
Couldn't they appeal to the authorities who, after all, gave them the land?
Bhelu said he went to the district magistrate after a public official told them to come by "if there is any problem."
But,
WHO WILL LISTEN TO US?
WE SPEND MONEY FROM OUR POCKET TO VISIT THEM, BUT NO ONE WILL LISTEN TO US...
I SPENT TEN RUPEES GOING TO AND FRO...
J. SACCO 6.10
They have sometimes refused to work the fields of the rajas and others who reappropriated the lands, but labor is too plentiful to make such boycotts meaningful.
"Ultimately," one of the Musahars admitted, "we work for them."
Do they think they'll ever get the land back?
"We hope for the best," we were told, "but it is a distant possibility. After all, he's king."
In fact, none of the rajas is king, but they have tied up the matter in court, and in India court proceedings might drag on for decades.
It seems the Musahars have been left with nothing.
WE ARE ALL LANDLESS LABORERS.

Meanwhile, we've arrived at one of three Hindu temples that Surendra wants to show us.
This one is to the goddess Durga.
कुलकुला देवी
The lower forms watch us intently.
They give me the creeps.
One of them runs up and snatches something from a vendor in front of the shrine.
On the way to the next temple, dedicated to the god Shiva, I notice a particularly scruffy Dalit peeling himself off from the other gawkers to follow us.
J. SACCO 6.10
Frankly, I don't like leaving my shoes at the entrance of each site—not with him standing around, anyway.

By the time we get to the shrine of the god Bhairav, I'm certain he's going to snatch my shoes.
But now he's following us over a wide, dusty area, and he seems more focused on Surendra than on me.
After a short ceremony at the tree, we head back to our shoes.
The young attendant positions himself behind Surendra,
who, with practiced ease,
raises one foot,
and then the other,
while the Dalit maneuvers the shoes for the raja to step into.
J. SACCO 4-10

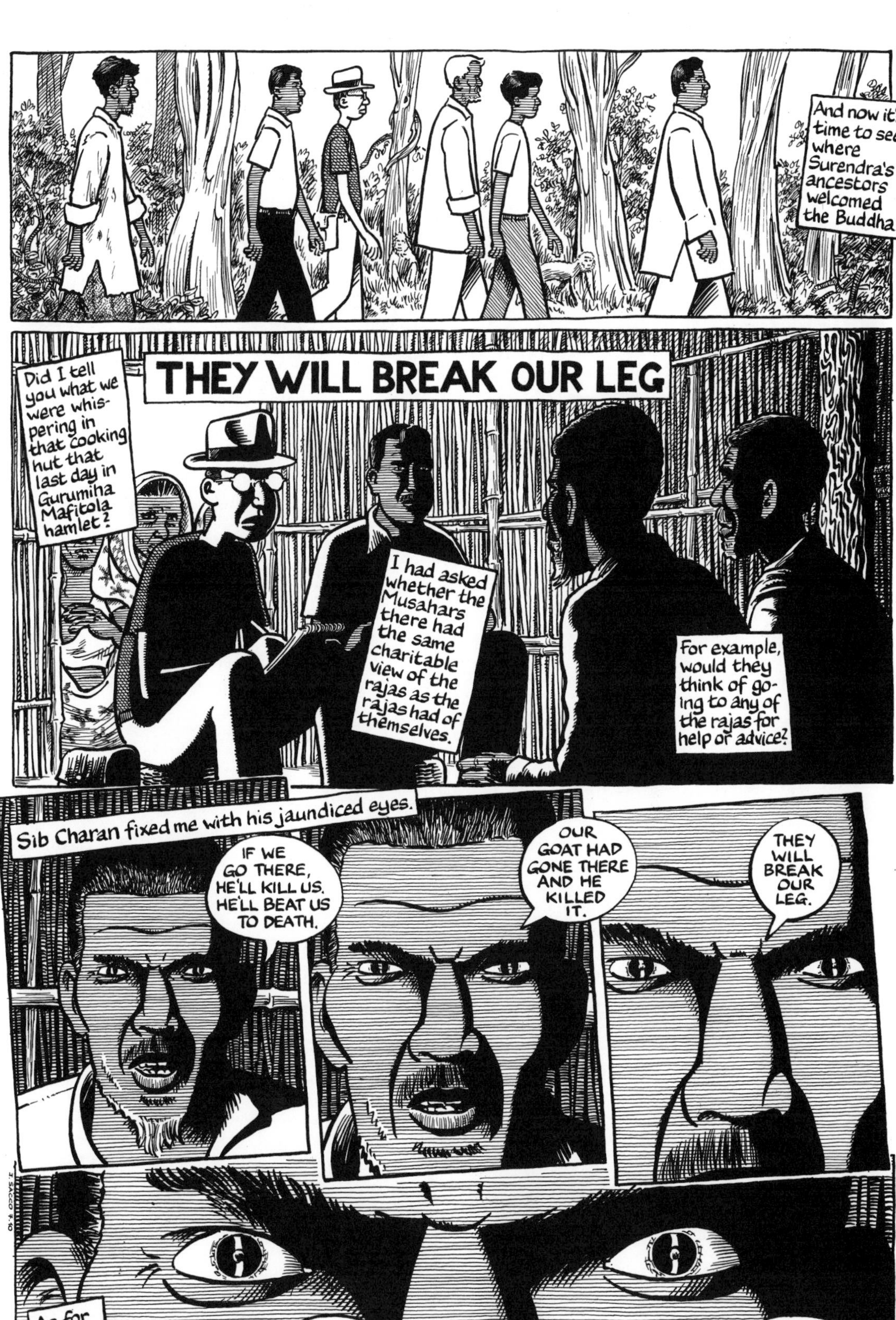
And now it's time to see where Surendra's ancestors welcomed the Buddha.
THEY WILL BREAK OUR LEG
Did I tell you what we were whispering in that cooking hut that last day in Gurumiha Mafitola hamlet?
I had asked whether the Musahars there had the same charitable view of the rajas as the rajas had of themselves.
For example, would they think of going to any of the rajas for help or advice?
Sib Charan fixed me with his jaundiced eyes.
IF WE GO THERE, HE'LL KILL US. HE'LL BEAT US TO DEATH.
OUR GOAT HAD GONE THERE AND HE KILLED IT.
THEY WILL BREAK OUR LEG.
As for working for the rajas,
THEY WILL NOT PAY US PROPERLY.
OH MY GOD, OH MY GOD, HE HAS THOUSANDS OF ACRES OF LAND, BUT STILL HE DOESN'T PAY.
AND IF WE ASK ANYTHING, THEY WILL KILL US.
THEY HAVE A BIG MANGO ORCHARD, BUT IF I PICK UP A SINGLE MANGO IT WILL BE FATAL FOR ME.

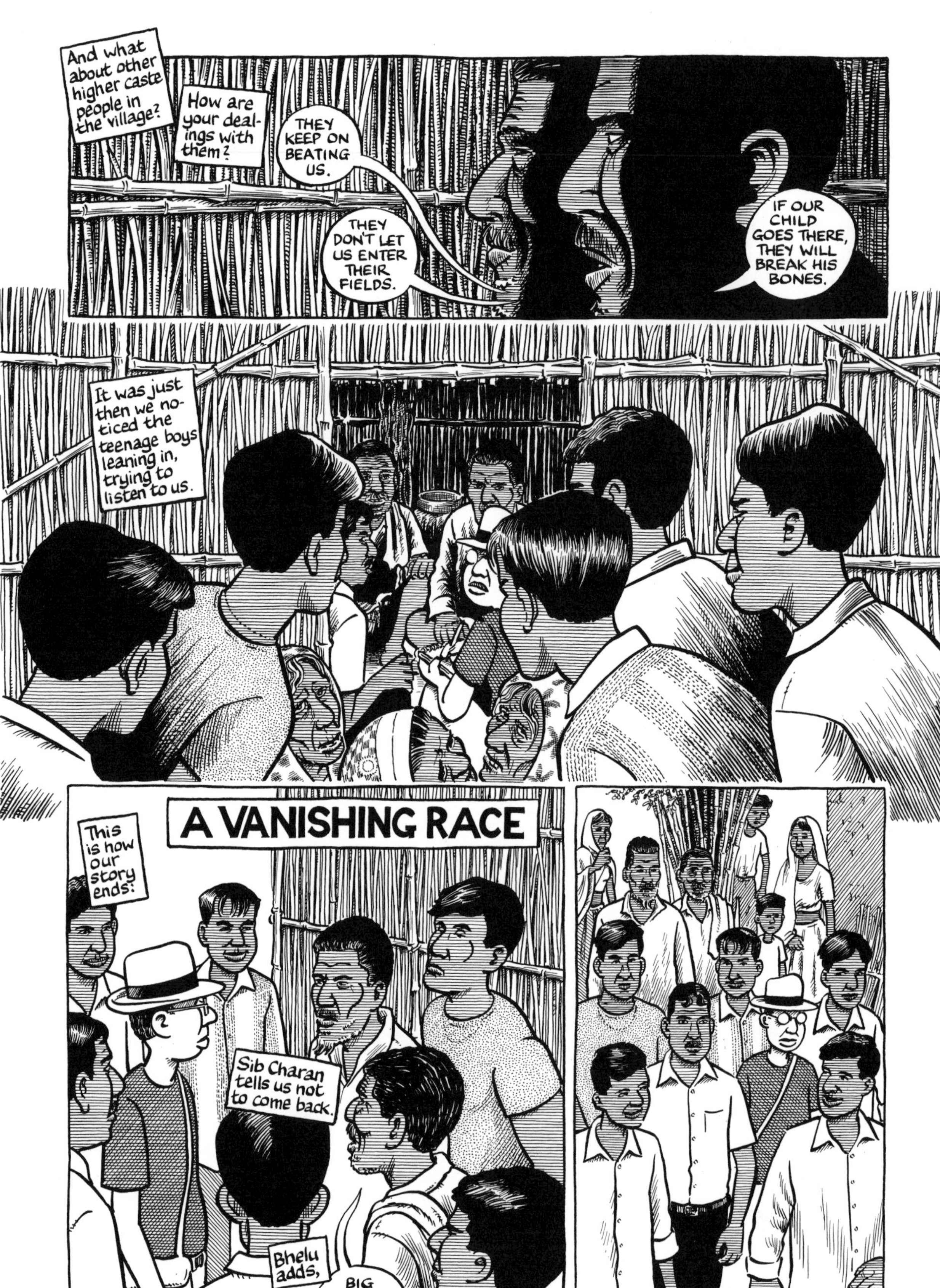
And what about other higher caste people in the village?
How are your dealings with them?
THEY KEEP ON BEATING US.
THEY DON'T LET US ENTER THEIR FIELDS.
IF OUR CHILD GOES THERE, THEY WILL BREAK HIS BONES.
It was just then we noticed the teenage boys leaning in, trying to listen to us.
A VANISHING RACE
This is how our story ends:
Sib Charan tells us not to come back.
Bhelu adds,
BIG PEOPLE WILL GET ANNOYED.
And those young, smirking boys, another generation of Green Shirts, escort us back to our car.
J. SACCO 7-10

As we pull away, I wonder how Dalits like these—
whose labor is all but superfluous,
whose only role seems to be attracting benefits that are easily plundered—
—can bust out of their dire circumstances.
I pose the question to Choudhary.
[WHEN] I WAS A POLITICAL ACTIVIST I USED TO TELL THEM TO EXERCISE THEIR POLITICAL RIGHTS AND ASSERT THEMSELVES, BUT NOW I DON'T SAY ANYTHING BECAUSE I KNOW WHENEVER THEY START RESISTING, THEIR SITUATION WILL FURTHER WORSEN.
THEY WILL BE ASSAULTED PHYSICALLY; THE POLICE WILL ARREST THEM...
WE CAN'T EXPECT THESE MOST POOR PEOPLE TO WAKE UP AND FIGHT AGAINST SUCH ODDS.
J. SACCO 7.10
But what will become of Sib Charan, his wife Suvanti, Bhelu, and the other Musahars we have met?
Choudhary tells me that Musahars, known for their association with rats, are "extreme Dalits" hated by other Dalits, who "practice untouchability with them."
I BELIEVE THEY ARE A VANISHING RACE... BECAUSE IN 62 YEARS OF INDEPENDENCE, THEIR SITUATION HAS GONE FROM BAD TO WORSE
WHAT WILL HAPPEN IN ANOTHER 62 YEARS?
IT APPEARS OBVIOUS THAT ALL OF THEM WILL BE DEAD AND THEY WILL BE PART OF HISTORY.

India, Notes

The extraordinarily successful French magazine *XXI*, which specializes in long-form narrative journalism and doesn't take advertisements, is the publishing industry's greatest champion of comics reportage. It has regularly sent cartoonists out into the world and given them a good deal of magazine space—thirty pages each. Editor Patrick de Saint-Exupery, a seasoned journalist himself, was open to any idea I had and supportive at every step of the way. Once I decided to draw a comic about poverty in India, the problem I had was narrowing my focus. I could have examined the notorious farmer suicides or the urban slums, but I wanted to get off the beaten track. The author Pankaj Mishra passed me along to Indian journalist Piyush Srivastava, who suggested I visit Kushinagar and who graciously agreed to be my guide. We met in Lucknow, where he is based, and drove for a day to reach the district, where many of the dalits—people regarded by many Indians as "untouchables"—are experiencing not just abject poverty but real hunger. My idea was to go to one village and get to know its inhabitants well over the course of a week or so. As detailed in the story, after three visits to the same hamlet, Piyush and I were essentially chased out of the area by higher caste individuals who did not like us snooping around. We decided to visit other villages, but briefly, for no more than a couple of hours each, to avoid the same result. I would have preferred not to do such hit-and-run journalism, but it was unavoidable under the circumstances and had the benefit of giving us a broader survey of conditions in the area.

"Kushinagar" appeared originally in French in *XXI*, no. 13, January/February/March 2011.

ACKNOWLEDGMENTS

This book encompasses stories from many trips to several countries over more than ten years and a full list of all those who have helped me along the way would go on for pages. Numerous journalists, fixers, translators, and others have schooled me, showed me how to be careful, and provided me with company and friendship. To them I am forever grateful.

But this time allow me to shift the focus away from colleagues in "the field" to acknowledge a few individuals who made a difference years before I got my first press pass. I am referring to certain teachers at Sunset High School in Portland, Oregon. (I had a few good professors in college too, but for me, as a whole experience, high school was more dense and intimate.)

I took my first journalism class from Brenda Holman. After she moved on, Sandra Ku took over. Both were superb instructors. I owe them a great debt for their encouragement and for instilling in me a love for rigorous news writing. They showed me that journalism was mostly fun and, when not quite fun, personally rewarding, which is how it has felt to me ever since, even under trying circumstances and even when the subject matter has been distasteful. Most important, they made me feel that good reporting mattered.

Hal Swafford was my history teacher. I didn't need to be convinced that history was interesting, but Mr. Swafford (I call him Hal now, but Mr. Swafford in this context sounds more appropriate) emphasized understanding the relationship between events rather than being able to recite them in the correct chronological order. "Think!" he used to command, tapping the side of his head, and he showed his students how. This book is dedicated to him and to Paul Copley, another esteemed teacher at Sunset High School, whose classes I never took but who entered my life decades later. Together with Hal and two Sunset grads, Rich LaSasso and Mike Stevens, I would meet Paul for drinks every few weeks at Cassidy's in downtown Portland. Those meetings brought out the best in us, I think, and in me certainly. There is no bullshitting ex–high school teachers like Hal and Paul, no saying a bunch of nonsense without being able to back it up with facts, and their opinion of me and my thoughts still matters terribly. Paul's passing was a real blow.

I also wish to thank my parents. I think they had misgivings about my studying journalism and even more misgivings when I seemed to give up journalism to draw comics. But they're proud of me now and see the value in what I do, and doesn't parental approval count as a victory in this world? Finally, I want to thank Amalie, who has put up with my long absences and never questioned my need to go places to see things. Leaving home with her heartfelt support has meant a great deal.

ABOUT THE AUTHOR

Joe Sacco, one of the world's greatest cartoonists, is widely hailed as the creator of war reportage comics. He is the author of, among other books, *Palestine*, which received the American Book Award, and *Safe Area Goražde*, which received the Eisner Award for best graphic novel and was named a *New York Times* Notable Book and *Time* magazine's best comic book of 2000. His most recent book, *Footnotes in Gaza*, was the first graphic novel to win the Ridenhour Book Prize, was short-listed for a *Los Angeles Times* Book Award, and also received an Eisner Award. Sacco's work has been translated into fourteen languages and his comics reporting has appeared in *Details*, *The New York Times Magazine*, *Time*, *Harper's*, and *The Guardian*, among other publications. He lives in Portland, Oregon.